STRAWBERRIES WITH THE FÜHRER

Strawberries with the Führer

A Journey from the Third Reich to New Zealand

Helga Tiscenko

SHOAL BAY PRESS

First published in 2000 by
Shoal Bay Press Ltd
Box 17-661,
Christchurch,
New Zealand

Copyright © 2000 Helga Tiscenko

ISBN 1 877251 03 8

Reprinted August 2000

Cover design by Communique Design

Cover photograph of Adolf Hitler by permission of
United States Holocaust Memorial Museum

Printed by Rainbow Print Ltd, Christchurch, New Zealand

Contents

Dedication

For Katerina, Mark and Tatjana,
    Sonja and Richard,
    Michael and Amanda,
who are the future

and in memory of Hermann and Elisabeth,
who are the past.

Acknowledgements

My sincere thanks to:
Owen Marshall, who encouraged me to write this story;
Anna Rogers, my editor, my friend, who dealt with the manuscript with empathy;
Ros Henry and David Elworthy of Shoal Bay Press, who put it all together;
my children and their partners, whose love and understanding I cherish;
and last, but by no means least,
to Nick, my husband and faithful companion for more than 50 years.

Note: Some names have been changed to protect individual identities.

Prologue

I sit on our terrace. It is a still and peaceful evening. The last rays of the sun slant through the trees and paint golden streaks on the grass of the paddock, and Indi, our old pony, stands near the water trough, content, dreaming. I, too, am dreaming. I, too, am content. Fate has been kind to me. Life has been good. Every day I can enjoy in New Zealand, my chosen country, is a blessing.

I belong here now. The days of homesickness for Germany, where I grew up, have passed, but the love for the country of my birth remains and is enriched by the love for this country, where my children grew up. But the memories are there, always.

This is my story. It is not meant to be a chronicle of my childhood during the Third Reich or a strict account of the early years in New Zealand. I did not keep diaries. I have written of incidents and feelings I experienced half a lifetime ago, as I remember them now.

It has not been an easy task. I have had to relive and come to terms with painful events of the past, open many a door in my mind that I had kept firmly shut all those years. It was safer that way then. Life demanded that I look forward, not back. But when my children had reached adulthood, they wanted to know, so I opened the doors for them. And now I open them for all of you who have asked me, 'What was it like for you?'

The stories in this book come from my heart. I state my own opinions. If these, and my recollections of events, conflict with those of my contemporaries here in New Zealand or in Germany, if my book gives offence or causes distress to anyone, I am truly sorry. It is my sincere hope that *Strawberries with the Führer* helps to dispel some prejudices and contributes to understanding between people of different origins, beliefs and views.

CHAPTER 1

Beginnings

The childhood photo of my mother, Elisabeth Schäfer, and her younger sister Rosel stands before me. It must have been taken in 1902; she seems to be four years old, Rosel about two. The little girls are seated behind a table, dressed in frilly white pinafores with broderie anglaise at necklines and sleeves. My mother's shoulder-length hair is wavy, caught up on top of her head by a white bow. Rosel's is straight, cut in a very short pageboy style, leaving her small left ear exposed. They were blonde at that time, although in later years both women had brunette hair, with auburn highlights. Rosel rests both arms on the table, one dimpled hand on top of the other. Elisabeth's left arm is also placed on the table, the hand slightly clenched, and her right hand appears protectively on Rosel's shoulder. They lean into each other, while facing the camera. Both have wide foreheads, straight noses, well-defined clefts in little chins, straight eyebrows over deep-set eyes. My mother's eyes are darker than Rosel's, her mouth more clearly defined, her lips fuller.

It must have been a formidable experience to have this portrait taken. Both little girls look tense and solemn, as if expecting something scary to happen. Rosel's expression conveys a hint of sadness and resignation, perhaps foreshadowing her tragic life?

Elisabeth and Rosel were fourth and fifth of five sisters and two brothers. Johanna, always called Hannejoh, was the eldest. Then came Maria, known as Rizebil, then Hans. After Elisabeth, Lis for short, and Rosel came Louise, called Lu, and finally Ludwig, or Ludda. I have been told they had a happy, if somewhat regimented childhood. All wore white sailor tunics in summer and navy blue sailor tunics in winter. Why the naval theme, nobody remembered; I suppose it was practical – one outfit could be handed down to the next child in line as they grew.

Offenbach, where my mother grew up, is quite an ordinary industrial city. It adjoins the much larger city of Frankfurt on the River Main. It has always been overshadowed by Frankfurt, but it has one claim to fame: it is the leather city of Germany. My mother's family were leather merchants and producers of leather goods, well-to-do, conservative and prolific. In old family photographs they look solemn, well mannered and neatly arranged, with a parent at each end and aspidistras as background. The family home, a four-storeyed, dark grey stone building of the style fashionable in the nineteenth century, with embellishments over the windows and columns adorning the front entrance, still looks solemn and well mannered, bearing with dignity the scars of Second World War bombing and the loss of its formal garden. It no longer belongs to the family and the seven children are all gone too.

All went well with the family in the early years of the twentieth century. The First World War did not have too much impact: both sons were too young to enlist and Opa (Grandpa) was indispensable to his factory. But the hungry years after the war and then the Depression affected them badly. The factory suffered, many workers had to be dismissed. There were protest marches and riots. The day 'The Mob' ran down their street, smashed their fence and hurled stones through the downstairs windows must have terrified the family. Many years later my mother and several of my aunts still talked about 'The Mob' with considerable emotion.

After the First World War the economic situation in Germany was grim, particularly in industrial cities like Offenbach, where unemployment was rife. My mother had completed her nursing training and was working at a children's crèche. Most of the children suffered malnutrition and had rickets; many died in the 1918 flu epidemic. I wonder if those experiences were one of the reasons why Elisabeth joined the Nazi Party in the mid-1920s.

I can write about the prevailing atmosphere of that period only by recollecting what I have been told. The citizens of Germany had been living under an authoritarian regime, the monarchy. They had been used to law and order and following the decrees issued by a stable government, largely without questioning. Patriotism, loyalty and obedience to the monarch, the church and the state were the order of the day. The same atmosphere prevailed in most European countries, including Britain, before and during the First World War.

From 1914 to 1918 German men had fought on the battlefields and in the trenches for their fatherland, just as their opponents had done for their mother country. The fighting was bitter and hard, but there was not, I think, the cruel

14

savagery that occurred in the Second World War. Be that as it may, the Germans saw the Treaty of Versailles, which followed the defeat and surrender of the German forces, as cruel, savage and unjust. Germany had to concede a large part of the Rhineland to France, a large part of Prussia to Poland and Bohemia and Moravia to the newly formed Czechoslovakian Republic. It had to pay huge sums in reparation. Steel production was outlawed, thus crippling heavy industry. The treaty had not only ensured that Germany could not be a world power or compete in world trade for a long time, it had also defeated and humiliated a proud people. They had fought and suffered in vain. Their values and beliefs were severely shaken. Their monarchy had disintegrated, the Kaiser had abdicated, their country was diminished in status and size. It must have been difficult to feel confidence in or allegiance to the government of the fledgling Weimar Republic, racked with scandals and the power struggles of diverse factions and political parties. The economy was shaky, inflation was out of control, there was widespread unemployment, poverty and hunger. There was profiteering and a black market. There was also the threat of communism, to which Germany's largest and most powerful neighbour, Russia, had succumbed. In 1919 there were communist uprisings in the capital, Berlin, in the industrial centres of the north-west, in Bremen and the Ruhr, even in conservative Munich. By 1923 the economy had collapsed completely and there were serious riots everywhere.

My parents, Hermann and Elisabeth, both 25 years old at this time, came from conservative families, whose values and living standards were now under threat. Hermann Höfle, who had had a strict Catholic upbringing, had volunteered for service in the First World War when he was 17. He had fought valiantly on the Western Front, had been decorated with the Iron Cross First Class and had risen to the rank of lieutenant. He decided to stay in the army at the end of the war, embarking on the career of a professional soldier in the 100,000 Mann Heer, the army of only 100,000 men permitted under the Treaty of Versailles. He loved his country and remained steadfast in his deep patriotic feelings to the day he died. In his view, communism was the great evil, the ultimate threat, and he fought against it all his life.

Elisabeth, who had been frightened by mob violence and who saw the effects of deprivation every day at the crèche, must have felt compassion for the suffering people around her and frustration about the unstable economic situation that she, her family and her charges had to endure.

Although the economy stabilised somewhat from 1924 to 1929, there must

15

still have been considerable dissatisfaction and unrest among the people. Adolf Hitler formed the National Socialist Party during that time. Nationalism had taken such a blow under the Treaty of Versailles that patriotic people were smarting. They were keen to 'put things right' again so nationalism became a popular concept. Socialism, justice for all, an egalitarian society that took care of all strata of society were equally appealing. National Socialism was also distinctly different from communism, which was international and 'proletarian', thereby threatening the very fabric of an ordered German society.

The Great Depression put an end to all hope of the re-establishment of a stable economy. By 1932 inflation had reached dizzying heights and unemployment figures had risen to six million. This crisis led to the rise of the right-wing movement of National Socialism, Hitler's party. Although he was unsuccessful in the 1932 presidential elections when he stood against Hindenburg, Hitler was made chancellor in January 1933, on the grounds that he would be best controlled inside the government.

My parents met and fell in love in Garmisch-Partenkirchen, a famous holiday resort in the German Alps, 90 kilometres south of Munich. It is surrounded by Germany's highest mountain range, which is not quite as high as the Southern Alps of New Zealand. The border between Austria and Germany runs along the summit of Germany's highest mountain, the Zugspitze (2965 metres). There is a restaurant on top from which one has a panoramic view of both the Austrian and Italian Alps and the ski-runs directly below. It is accessible by a little rack railway and cable car from the valley floor of Garmisch. There is usually enough snow in the Garmisch area for cross-country and downhill skiing during the winter months. The 1936 Winter Olympics took place there.

In spring, summer and autumn holidaymakers still flock to Garmisch to go hiking, a sport much beloved by most city dwellers, to go rock climbing, to enjoy the mountain air and sunshine, or simply to relax and imbibe in the many hotels, sanatoria, restaurants and cafés. In spite of the number of modern buildings, Garmisch manages to preserve the atmosphere of a typical Bavarian alpine village. Most of the houses are adorned by frescoes, wooden balustrades on balconies with flower-boxes and wooden shingles on their roofs festooned with rows of flat boulders to keep the snow from sliding down in heavy chunks during a thaw.

The locals wear the traditional Bavarian dress, called the Tracht. Lederhosen (leather pants), Lodenjanker (felted jacket) and of course the hat with a

My mother's family, c.1918. From left: Maria, Hans, little Ludwig (Ludda), Rosel, Johanna (Hannejoh), Elisabeth (Lis, my mother) and, in front, Luise (Lu).

Lis and her sister Rosel.

Lis in nurse's uniform, 1920.

My parents Lis and Hermann Höfle on their wedding day, 20 November 1920.
My father is in the dress uniform of an officer in the 100,000 Mann Heer.

Opa Schäfer, just as I remember him.

An outing with Opa Schäfer and Mutti in Munich, 1931.

With Oma Höfle, 1932. Perhaps I was going off to spend a night in one of her wonderful Federbetten?

Posing for a family photo after the arrival of my sister Sigrid.

Photos of the time show me looking less than enthusiastic about the new baby because she took up a lot of Mother's time, but I enjoyed being Daddy's big girl.

A portrait taken at about the time I met Adolf Hitler (left). This is probably the blue dress I recall wearing on that occasion! With Mutti (right).

Gamsbart (brush) or, particular to the Garmisch region, an Adlerflaum (eagle-down feather) for the men. For the women, the Dirndl, with a low-cut, tight-fitting bodice, puffed sleeves and a gathered skirt topped by an apron is de rigueur. As the Tracht looks attractive and has an air of healthy outdoor country living, it is eagerly bought and worn by most tourists who come to Bavaria.

Lis and her best friend Trudl, who later became my godmother, were holi-daying with a party of nurses in a chalet near the Kreuzeck at the foot of the Alpspitz. Hermann was on furlough, visiting his uncle, the Oberförster (chief forester) of Garmisch, to do a bit of climbing and hunting. The young couple met during a thunderstorm. My father endeared himself to the ladies by chiv-alrously carrying them one by one piggyback through the rain and mud from the Kreuzeck hotel to their chalet so that they did not ruin their dancing shoes. According to mother, they all had their eyes on him and invited him to call the next day. He did and asked Lis, and Lis only, to accompany him on a Bergtour, a mountain walk. Trudl and the others were disappointed.

Opa liked Hermann and Lis's whole family accepted the engagement with pleasure. Not so pleased was Hermann's mother, Oma (Grandma) Höfle. A devout Catholic, she resented her only son's decision to marry a Ketzerin (her-etic), a Protestant. When Hermann became very ill with a burst appendix she declared it to be God's punishment for the engagement. It was not until years later that Hermann forgave his mother that remark. In time she got on very well with her daughter-in-law and was a devoted grandmother to my sister and me.

Their wedding photo, on 20 November 1925, shows Lis in a stylish, long-waisted three-quarter-length dress, white long gloves and stockings, pointed shoes to match, a long tulle veil fastened to the band of rosebuds encircling her forehead. She looks soft and beautiful. Hermann is resplendent in full dress uniform. His long riding boots with spurs are so elegantly tight that he must have found it difficult to walk in them. His ring hand holds the long ceremonial sword and his collar is so high that there is hardly any room for the chin-strap holding the helmet in place. It comes down to his eyebrows and seems too big for him. On the left side of the tunic is a large band of military decorations from the First World War, the Iron Cross holding pride of place over his heart. He appears self-assured and determined, but they both look young and vulnerable.

The newly-weds made their home in Munich in the Borstei, a modern apart-ment block mostly occupied by families attached to the armed forces. Hermann had been promoted to first lieutenant of the 9th Artillery Company. The first few years of their marriage saw very uncertain and turbulent times and they were faced with many difficult decisions. Hermann was the more dominant partner and his strong patriotic views probably influenced my mother to a decisive extent.

Bitterly disappointed by the political climate of the post-war years, Hermann belonged to the Freicorps (free corps) actively opposing Prime Minister Friedrich Ebert's government. When and how my parents became attracted to the National Socialist Party I do not know, but Hermann's moment of truth had come when Hitler and his followers marched to the Feldherrn Halle, the war memorial at the end of the Ludwigstrasse in Munich, on 9 November 1923. The army had been ordered to prevent the march from reaching the Feldherrn Halle and Hermann and his men were stationed in a recess of the wall surrounding the Hofburg Gardens, machine guns ready to open fire. When the marchers approached he recognised some of his friends among them so he and his men abandoned their post and joined the march. The machine gun on the opposite side of the road did fire upon the marchers, killing several.

'I could not open fire on my comrades,' said Hermann at the court martial. The march on the Feldherrn Halle ended in bloodshed and failure, but the Nazi Party had its first martyrs. Hitler was imprisoned in the Fortress Landsberg where he wrote *Mein Kampf.* The party was outlawed and went underground but, in spite of this, gained popularity and momentum.

Although Hermann retained his position in the army, lean and precarious times followed for him and Elisabeth before Hitler was elected Reichskanzler (Chancellor of the Republic) in 1933. Hermann was then awarded the Blut Orden (Blood Order), the prestigious order worn only by participants in the ill-fated march to the Feldherrn Halle. Elisabeth received the Goldenes Partei Abzeichen (Golden Party Insignia) as one of the earliest party members. With this they sealed their fate. They swore the oath of allegiance to Hitler; he became their Führer (leader) to whom they were faithful right to the bitter end.

I cannot understand how my parents, two decent and intelligent people, could ignore all the signs pointing to Hitler's madness and megalomania. How they could turn a blind eye to the manifestations of racial hatred that led to the Holocaust, how they could swallow all that nonsense of the Arisches Blut (Aryan pure blood) and how they could reconcile their personal compassionate actions with those of a callous regime, responsible for the suffering and death of millions of people.

There must have been conflict in their hearts and minds. I can only suppose that adherence to that code of honour, 'Deutsche Treue' (German faithfulness), prevented them from dissenting. It seems so futile and incomprehensible to me now. The conflict of loving my parents and yet knowing that they were followers of an ideology I reject remains forever in my heart. This is a burden I have in common with many Germans of my generation.

The march to the Feldherrn Halle was commemorated every year in November by those who had taken part. They marched in order of merit, my father in the ninth row. I remember seeing him march past my mother and me when we attended the memorial service and feeling puzzled and tearful when I was shown the place where he sat behind sandbags in his machine-gun nest, waiting to shoot his friends.

This childhood incident left such a lasting impression on me that I found myself unable to talk about it to my daughter Sonja. We were standing in the Hofburg Gardens in 1985, 40 years after the Second World War and the end of the Nazi Party. For her it was history – she wanted to know what happened, what part her grandfather had played – but for me it was still the unresolved pain of reconciling the beliefs of my parents, whom I loved dearly, and of my childhood ideals which proved to be so false.

Hermann and Elisabeth had been married for four years before I came along. I was born at 11 a.m. on 26 September 1929, on my mother's birthday. Lis had had an easy pregnancy and kept very fit; I am told she swam her usual 10 lengths of the pool the day before I arrived. Hermann was convinced that he would get a son. As usual, the military band was playing its Sunday repertoire on the lawn in front of the hospital. Fathers to be, in those days, paced the corridor, while babies were delivered behind closed doors. My father, upon being told the birth was imminent, raced downstairs to the conductor: 'Please, play the Radetzky March, my wife is just giving birth to our son!' When he arrived, out of breath, at the delivery room again, the doctor poked his head out the door and congratulated him on a healthy daughter. I am told my father staggered to the nearest window, leaned out, waved his arms and croaked, 'A waltz, a waltz, it's a girl!'

CHAPTER 2

Grandparents

Grandmother Schäfer's family were French gentry. As Huguenots, they had been forced to flee to Germany and settle there, but Grandmother never forgot her French origins. The only glimpse of her still in my memory is of a lady with dark brown hair arranged in folds on top of her head who wore a grey silk dress that rustled. She sat very upright in a cane chair, holding out her hand. 'Bonjour, Grandmère', with a curtsey and a brushing of her hand with one's lips was the morning greeting she expected of her grandchildren. She must have died when I was quite young.

The only other family member from 'the French connection' who played a role in my childhood memories was Aunt 'Non-non'. Although her real name was Louise, we called her 'Non-non' because that was her standard reply to almost any question she was asked. The simple reason for this negativity? She could neither speak nor understand German, a language she refused to waste her time learning, although this was no obstacle at all to a very happy marriage to her German husband. Uncle Jo was a popular and respected solicitor and notary public in a smallish Bavarian town, whose residents took his eccentric French wife to their collective ample bosoms.

The shopkeepers even put up with Non-non's French habit of poking at their wares with a well-manicured finger, to test the freshness of vegetables and meat. This always amazed and embarrassed me when she took me on her shopping expeditions. Aunt Non-non was a tall, slender and elegant figure – dark, later greying, hair looped back into a chignon, expressive black eyes, a generous mouth with very white teeth that often flashed an amused smile.

In her drawing room was a floor-to-ceiling Kachelofen (tiled stove) imported from her homeland. It was a work of art, decorated all over in blue and white tiles depicting village scenes and people of medieval times and floral borders.

Aunt Non-non's cooking was intriguingly foreign to me. Sautéed lettuce leaves in a garlic and sour cream sauce were delicious, as were her dainty savoury pastries, but I could never bring myself to sample her escargots (vineyard snails), which had to be winkled out of their shells with a special instrument, to be consumed by those with more flair, or a sturdier constitution, than I possessed. Aunt Non-non lived in Germany right through the turbulent times of the Second World War, staunchly French, totally unperturbed and unmolested.

My maternal grandfather, Heinrich Schäfer, lived to 83 and is still very much alive in my memory: a faint scent of the slender cigarillos he used to smoke, the scratchiness of his coat sleeves as his arms cradled me, bright reflections on his polished shoes and the soft, waxy feel of his beard. Ah, his beard – snowy white and wavy and long enough for me to plait a red ribbon into. I did a lot of plaiting. I had to keep my fingers busy to stop the lump in my throat and the ache in my chest from getting unbearable whenever he told me my favourite story of 'Faithful Hans' again and again. Hans, the beautiful brave white horse, saved his equally beautiful brave young rider from dying on the battlefield by carrying him to safety, although he was mortally wounded himself: 'Their blood mingled as it flowed over his white flanks ...' My grandfather had many stories, but Hans was the best and I never tired of hearing it.

I also loved looking at the things from Grandfather's past. His business had taken him to the steppes of Russia many times to buy pelts and hides and his huge fur coat and hat, smelling deliciously of camphor, were kept in an upstairs wardrobe. If you succeeded in wrestling the coat from its hanger, you could hide in it and pretend you were in a tent or a cave.

Sometimes he showed us grandchildren the other treasures from the wardrobe. His fur boots which reached way up beyond your knees, so that you walked awkwardly with stiff legs and splayed feet when you tried them on. His money belt, soft leather with buckles and many pockets that had held real gold roubles. And his pistol, long-barrelled with his initials etched into silver plates on each side of the hammer, now resting on its purple velvet bed securely locked in its wooden case. According to Grandfather, it had been used 'to fend off wolves and bandits'. Our favourite of these wonderful relics was the forbidden treasure, the sword-stick. We were never allowed to touch it, 'because it's so deadly', we told each other in whispers and of course we touched it as a dare. It rested among umbrellas and the other ordinary walking sticks in a brass tube in the hall, pretending to be just one of them. Only the silver handle distinguished it: an animal shape, half scaly fish, half snarling beast of

21

prey. Twist and pull the handle and out flashed a long, thin, sharp, deadly blade. I once cut my index finger on it and it hurt and it bled and I cried and was terrified. But my grandfather only said, 'Now you know', tied a thick bandage round my finger and fed me brandied cherries to make it all better again.

My father's family lived in Augsburg, the old Reichs Stadt (Imperial city), which has a 2000-year-old history, having been founded by the Roman Emperor Augustus. (Augsburg is short for Augustus Burg, the fort of Augustus.) A part of the Roman fortification wall still stands next to Augsburg's Dom or cathedral. A thriving trading centre in medieval times, the city can boast the oldest retirement complex in Europe, the Fuggere'. It was founded in the 16th century by wealthy merchants, the Fugger family, to house their faithful staff when they had reached the age of retirement. The oldies paid a peppercorn rent to live out their lives in pleasant little cottages arranged around a tree-lined square within a walled complex in the middle of the city. The Fuggerei still houses a number of the city's pensioners, who pay the same amount of rent established 500 years ago.

I do not have much information about my father's family. The few relations I have met lived in the countryside surrounding Augsburg; the family name, Höfle, means small farm. My paternal grandfather might have been the first to move into the city. Hermann, my father, was an only child. As far as I know, he grew up in the city; he certainly went to school in Augsburg.

Opa Höfle, who had been the chief postmaster of the city, died when I was a baby. I am told he dangled his gold pocket watch like a pendulum back and forth above the basket in which I lay and chuckled with delight when my small fist grasped the watch. 'She'll make good use of her time,' he predicted. To me, Opa Höfle was an angel. Wings outspread, face uplifted, hands grasping a palm frond, forever heaven bound – that's how I saw him, on the marble monument towering over the family plot in the cemetery we visited every day when staying with Oma Höfle. Secretly I hoped that he would not be there at our next pilgrimage to his grave, that his marble pedestal would be empty, that he would have taken off during the night and made his flight to heaven. But he never did.

Oma Höfle always said a prayer at Opa's grave, for the repose of his soul, at the end of which she crossed herself and taught my sister and me to genuflect too. 'She goes there to repent – she led him an awful life' was my father's somewhat cynical response to this ritual. 'The Holy Sunday Rows' between his parents were vivid childhood memories for him. Oma wore shapeless ankle-length dresses with a lorgnette on a long chain dangling somewhere between ample bosom and waist. She used to lift the lorgnette to her right eye when surveying vendors on market stalls or examining merchandise and before fishing out the correct change from her pouch purse. 'Just for effect. She can see perfectly well,' said my father. It certainly worked – she looked quite formidable when using her lorgnette and any attempt to outsmart her was surely nipped in the bud.

Oma lived on the third floor of the apartment building she owned, one of a row of identical solid grey stone houses, with double-glazed windows and heavy oak doors. They rose straight from the Bürgersteig (footpath) and faced the cemetery where Opa's grave was situated. Her life had set routines. Every Wednesday she and her cronies played Skat (cards) at the corner pub. They met at their Stammtisch (reserved table), drank Malzbier (stout) and ate Weisswurst (white sausage) with Bretzen (pretzels) while playing – for money! Every Saturday evening she went to confession and early Sunday morning to mass. After the service Opa got fresh flowers put into the stone urn at the pedestal of the angel and had his grave tidied up. She carried a special little trowel and brush in an embroidered hold-all for this purpose. Sometimes I was allowed to brush over the gold lettering on his headstone.

When staying with Oma we slept in Federbetten (feather beds). The eiderdown duvets underneath and on top made you sink into a warm nest from which it was difficult to see or climb out. Oma warmed our beds with big oval copper containers filled with boiling hot water. They had to be removed before you got into bed 'or you'll scald your feet'. Then you snuggled into the deliciously hot patches the 'hotties' left behind.

One year my sister and I stayed with Oma during the Easter holidays. On Palm Sunday we went to church with her, each carrying a beribboned bunch of Weidenkätzle (pussywillow) branches. There are no palm leaves available at the end of a Northern Hemisphere winter! After the service, she sprinkled us and our willow branches with holy water and then, when we got home, she made us eat a catkin. 'Now you will not get a sore throat all year,' she announced triumphantly, after we had swallowed the hairy things. Superstition? Well, I suppose if you managed to get a medium-sized hairy catkin past your tonsils, they were in pretty good shape anyway, with or without the blessing.

Oma had big linen cupboards made of dark inlaid wood, standing on ball feet and closed with wrought iron locks. Inside were shelf after shelf of beautifully embroidered tablecloths, sheets, pillowcases, duvet covers and towels tied with silk ribbon, kept fragrant by sachets of rose petals and lavender. She never used these linen parcels, which stayed in their cupboards all her married life. 'Part of my dowry,' she told us. 'I'll pass these on to you when you get married.'

It never came to pass. Poor Oma died of cancer in the summer of 1945. Distant cousins had told her just before she died that her only son, my father, and all his family had perished so she willed all she owned to them. They may have acted in good faith at the time and, having been bombed out, could certainly make good use of Oma's estate. It was sad, though, that they were unwilling to share at least part of Oma's wealth with us, when it turned out that we had not perished.

When my mother made her way to Augsburg in the autumn of 1945, hoping for some support from Oma, she had died and been buried beside Opa, her apartment was let to strangers and the cousins were not very sympathetic to my mother's plight. About 30 years later, their adopted son got in touch with my sister. He had been informed by the Augsburg City Council that a motorway was being constructed through cemetery land. The owners of family plots were to be compensated and their wishes about the disposal of monumental masonry respected. It appeared that Opa's angel had been sculpted by a well-known artist and was worth a tidy sum. The son, a nice, decent guy who had become a lawyer, had then researched the family history and found my sister. They met, shared a glass of wine, decided to sell the angel and split the proceeds. Poor Opa Höfle, I wonder if he is gazing heavenward on somebody else's grave now.

Opa and Oma Höfle, good Catholics that they were, sent my father to a school run by Benedictine monks who wore long brown robes, white cords knotted round their middles and sandals on their bare feet. When they walked sedately along the stone-flagged passages, their sandals and robes made a swish-flopping sound which so enchanted my father that he decided he too would become a monk when he grew up. This pious wish was warmly welcomed by the Benedictines; I wonder what they thought when he became a general instead.

Whether he received a well-rounded education there I cannot tell, but he certainly learned Latin and discipline and developed an irreverent sense of humour and a love for music that gave him pleasure all his life. He was an accomplished pianist and organist and whenever the opportunity arose, he went into a church to play the organ, mostly Bach and Händel. Often I functioned as his bellows boy, feet pedalling on two narrow boards, up and down, up and down, while hanging on to a bar for dear life. It was quite taxing, since I had to pedal moderately fast or furiously fast, according to the tempo and volume of the score.

While at school, he had been organist for the two Sunday morning services. By the time he had played through the repertoire for the second time, he told me with a twinkle in his eye, he was bored and often played the last piece extra fast so that the congregation had to gallop through their Hallelujahs and he could go. In spite of his devotion to Hitler and his National Socialist doctrine, my father retained a close relationship with the Catholic church and it with him. It was a contradiction but this was the time when Clerical Fascism was in vogue.

This term referred to the attitude of the Catholic church towards Hitler's Germany, Franco's Spain and Mussolini's Italy. All these fascist regimes were fiercely opposed to communism which, with its atheistic ideology and opposition to the established social order, threatened the very existence of the church. Under communist regimes, religious activity was not only forbidden, but persecuted. Although in effect so very close to its deadly enemy, communism, fascism was perceived to be the bulwark against the revolutionary forces of Bolshevism. The slogan of fascism, 'Credere, obedire, combatere' (have faith, obey, fight), could equally well apply to a militant Christian church, the church of the Crusaders, the Knights Templar, the Teutonic knights, the Conquistadores of Latin America, the Inquisition …

CHAPTER 3

Berlin

My parents moved from Munich to Berlin in 1932, when I was three. The shift was related to my father's career in the army. I am not sure what his rank or position was, but I remember him looking very handsome in his field-grey uniform with long, black, tight-fitting boots. He may have risen to the rank of captain about that time; he was definitely mounted, as army officers were in those days. He had a chestnut horse called Rudi and sometimes he lifted me up into the saddle. It was utter bliss, high on horseback, being led at a sedate pace along the bridle paths of the Tiergarten, the big park right in the middle of the city.

We lived in an apartment on the third floor of a large grey apartment block in a tree-lined street, Albrecht Strasse 38, in Steglitz. There was no garden, so we went for walks, feeding the many pigeons that lived in the park and in the winter we went tobogganing in the Tiergarten. When I was four and a half years old, on 15 April 1934, my sister Sigrid was born. I must have been a trifle jealous of the new arrival: photos of this period show me with a less than delighted expression when I am close to the baby.

My parents probably felt that it would be good for me to have my own living creature to love and care for – Peter the teddy bear no longer sufficed – so, to my great joy, I was given a pet rabbit. He grew into a large brownish grey buck and I called him Fürst (Duke). He had his hutch on the balcony outside my window and could jump in and out of the bedroom at will. One day, however, he jumped in the wrong direction. Over the railings he went and plummeted three storeys to land on the concrete of the back yard. By the time I had raced down the stairs, tearful and screaming, he was sitting up and sneezing. A bit of blood trickled out of his nose, he had broken his right hind leg and I guess he had a headache too, because he was very cross and bit me when I picked him up. He was fine after the vet had put his leg in plaster.

Fürst had to have his leg replastered three times because he fractured his cast whenever he thumped his leg in anger, which was often. He thumped in rage when the sparrows stole his rabbit pellets, he thumped with frustration when I closed his hutch at night, he thumped in defiance when I tried to winkle him out from under my bed, he thumped when he was brushed – he really was a very bad-tempered rabbit. But I loved him and cried when he died at the ripe old age of five. His big funeral, attended by several of my friends, was quite good fun really: we decorated his grave with coloured marbles and all the mourners had ice cream and chocolate cake afterwards.

The first of a succession of dogs that so enriched my life joined our family shortly after Fürst's demise. Much beloved, Waldi I, a short-haired black Dachshund, came everywhere with us. In fact he was always the first into the car whenever we went on an outing and we children found it difficult to get into the back seat, where Waldi's long form was already sprawled. One day my father put Waldi up on the folded canvas roof of the car while we were loading it and we forgot about him curled up asleep on top. When we rounded the corner at the end of our street, Waldi fell off, sailing past our horrified eyes to land in a bush by the side of the road. We screeched to a halt, just touching a lamp-post, but fortunately Waldi had only a scratched nose.

Waldi had just one failing, a passion for hunting fox and badger. It was in his genes: Dachshund means badger dog and the short, crooked front legs are perfect for digging. He dived into every hole he came across in the hope of finding his quarry and he stayed below for hours. The family, anxious ears to the ground, followed his progress through the warren as muffled yips and yaps indicated his location. A badger or fox, cornered in his lair, will fight to kill and our Waldi, much smaller than his prey, was in peril. We always carried a spade in the boot of the car and my father spent many a harrowing hour digging frantically into the warrens where Waldi did battle. Sometimes he was lucky enough to dig at the right spot and would haul Waldi out by his hind leg, or tail – 'Just in time!' we breathed in relief – but most times Waldi's battle raged just ahead of the hole my father had dug. 'Over here, quickly!' we would yell and he dug again. And again. I remember him uttering dire threats, such as 'giving the dog a good hiding', or leaving him down there – 'serve him right if he was mauled' – but whenever Waldi finally emerged, he was lovingly examined for injuries, brushed clean of dirt, cuddled and bundled back into the car.

Our first car was a dashing dark blue convertible with a long running board, two spare tyres mounted on the boot and a canvas roof folded right down. Alas, it did not always unfold quickly to cover us in sudden showers, but we certainly looked rather sporty and fashionable going for a drive wearing white linen caps and goggles.

My baby sister took up a lot of my mother's time and I enjoyed being Daddy's big girl. I was sometimes allowed to go with him to his office at the army barracks. It was fun to sit on the swivel chair which was wound up high so that I could tap on the typewriter. It was fun to watch the soldiers come and go, saluting and clicking their heels as they did so. One day there must have been some trouble because I heard my father say that he had to 'sort out his staff'. When they were assembled and standing at attention, he became aware of me sitting in a corner on my swivel chair, all eyes and ears. To his request to get down and go outside to play I replied, 'But Daddy, I want to watch you sort out your staff!' They smirked, he lost his momentum and I was not invited to the office for a long time.

From 1934 to 1940 several career opportunities presented themselves to my father. At this time the German government was on very friendly terms with Generalissimo Chiang Kai-Shek, presumably because the Chinese leader was fighting against the common enemy, the communists. The fact that Chiang's wife was of Viennese origin might also have played a role. My father had been groomed to become military adviser to Chiang and had got as far as packing his trunk and making arrangements for us to follow him to China, when the appointment was cancelled. He must have been very disappointed. I can still see him, holding a fur boot in each hand, saying, 'Damn, all that for nothing!'

Heinrich Himmler wanted my father to join the Schutzstaffel, the SS, and he came for dinner one evening to discuss this prospect. I remember him as a shortish, round-faced man with bristly, mousy hair. He wore a grey tunic. We ate spaghetti bolognese, Himmler's favourite dish, and he was very friendly and jolly and wanted me to sit on his knee, but I squirmed away; I did not like him – his glasses glittered. My parents probably did not like him either, because my father declined his offer and went off to the Spanish Civil War instead.

Many of my childhood memories of the 1933-1939 period are fragmented and hazy, but one is as clear as if it had happened yesterday. I remember the day my mother and I went to the parade in Berlin at Unter den Linden, the wide street leading through the Siegestor, the monumental Brandenburg Gate surmounted by a bronze sculpture of Winged Victory driving a quadriga. It was springtime and the military parade celebrated Hitler's birthday on 20 April.

I was wearing a light blue dress with a shiny white collar, frilled at the edges, and new T-bar sandals that pinched a bit. I stood between lots of legs and finally right on the edge of the pavement in front of everybody else so that I could see. There were long red flags billowing down from tall buildings across the wide street. It was very bright and hot and exciting – and noisy.

When the planes screamed overhead I had to cover my ears and screw up my eyes. When the huge tanks clanged past, the ground shook and I hid behind and held onto the big leg nearest to me, peeping out and up to the brave soldiers, who looked so handsome with their straight arms resting on the sides of the open hatch and their bronzed faces looking straight ahead and their dark berets straight on top of their heads. I wanted a beret like that!

The battalions marched past in columns so wide that they filled the street. Their black boots rose and fell in lines, the bright light reflected in the shiny leather. Their arms were held out rigidly as they saluted, line after line, column after column. The roar of the crowd lining the pavement rose and fell: 'Sieg Heil, Sieg Heil!' And my voice rose and fell too and I got a big lump in my throat and I felt so proud, because my father was there too. I could not see him among all those lines, but I knew he was there, marching straight and tall.

Later, carefully carrying a bouquet of forget-me-nots, I climbed up the white marble steps of the Reichskanzlei (Chancellery) beside my mother. Up, up through the high double portals and on and on. There were many people and there was He, the Führer, right in front of me! And I could not say the words of the birthday greeting I had learnt by heart. I held the forget-me-nots up to him and he took them and he had the brightest, bluest eyes.

'Thank you,' he said. He kissed me lightly on the cheek, told me they were his favourite flowers and asked if I would like to eat some strawberries with cream. 'Not with cream, but with ice cream, please,' I whispered and felt myself going red as everybody laughed. But the Führer did not laugh at me. He sat down beside me and we ate strawberries and vanilla ice cream together and I did not spill anything on my blue dress and if he had asked me to die for him there and then I would have done so, unquestioningly.

CHAPTER 4

Before the War

After my father's return from the Spanish War, it must have been in 1937 or 1938, we moved to Berlin-Lichterfelde West, a more upmarket suburb, adjacent to Dahlem, which was regarded as the best area in those days. We rented the ground floor of a two-storeyed villa at Kyllmannsstrasse 7.

The house belonged to Mr Holz, an old gentleman who had made his fortune as a goldminer in Australia. Not only did he have a large gold nugget on the chain of his pocket watch, he could also shout 'Cooee' piercingly, thereby proving that he had indeed lived an adventurous life down under. The villa stood in a big garden, backing onto the house of the film star and director, Leni Riefenstahl. In the second-floor apartment lived the director of the Berlin State Opera, Ernst Legal. He and my father became good friends and often played duets on the Steinway grand piano that was my father's pride and joy. Our respective housekeepers, however, had no friendly feelings towards each other, and furtive animosity and competition were rampant on the back stairs.

Along the front of the house ran a glassed-in verandah, the Wintergarden, where, in the jungle of large indoor plants, we played cowboys and Indians. I was always the Noble Indian, by merit of owning two important props: an Indian costume, complete with feathered head-dress, and my rocking horse, which was covered with real horse hide and had a real horse's tail. (Lesser rocking horses had fake fur and rope tails.)

One morning Leni Riefenstahl had burglars. Armed police came with sirens wailing and surrounded her house, there was much shouting through loud-hailers and lots of men scurried through our garden. We watched with fascinated horror from the attic window. For once Sophie, 'Ernst Legal's Dragon' as we called her in loyalty to our Helene, stood amiably beside Helene, absorbed in watching the drama unfold. We heard shots but, much to our disappointment, it was only tear gas exploding. There was no bloodshed, the five burglars came out, meek and mild, and were bundled into the Black Maria.

Leni Riefenstahl was not a nice neighbour. Every time our two pet tortoises ambled through the fence to sample her lettuces, she rang up and complained, and once she even *threw* the poor darlings back over the fence. Maria and Maritza Tortoise led exciting lives. The size of pudding plates, they had travelled from Yugoslavia on a bed of hay in the boot of my father's car. Upon release they were determined to walk back to their homeland, but as they were rather slow and ponderous and needed frequent stops for rest and refreshments, they were usually retrieved before they got out of the gate. Only once did they make it halfway across the street where Maritza was run over by a van. Fortunately she had a very hard shell and the only harm done was to the claws of her right front foot. Mari and Maritza hibernated successfully in a wooden box filled with hay and wood chips and we enjoyed their company for almost two years. Then, during a cold snap in autumn, they secretly dug their way into winter quarters of their own design in the compost heap and that was their undoing. Next spring we discovered two little tortoise shells at the bottom of the heap.

During these years our parents frequently went out to evening functions: operas, concerts and the theatre. Tucked up in bed, my little sister and I always insisted on being sung to sleep before they went, so, resplendent in evening dress, they sang 'Guten Abend, gute Nacht' (Brahms' Lullaby) and 'Der Mond ist aufgegangen' (The moon has risen) before kissing us goodnight. Two of my mother's evening gowns were particularly beautiful. One, in a black and white classical style, we had named 'Haile Selassie' after the Ethiopian Emperor who had just visited Berlin; the other gown of a shimmering light blue was 'The Holy Ghost'.

When I was eight I started piano lessons with Papa Steiner, who lived a few houses along the street. He had several sons, all very talented musicians, and one of them, Max, became famous writing and performing music for Hollywood's film industry. Papa Steiner was a kindly and patient man. He taught me to keep level and steady over the keyboard by putting a raspberry sweet on the back of each hand. If the sweet did not fall off as I played my piece, I could eat it afterwards. He instilled a love of music in me, taught me to pick a note and sing in tune but, much to his disappointment, I did not have enough talent to become a famous musician like his son.

Having suffered from tummy aches on and off for a few months, I was diagnosed as having a grumbling appendix. 'Out with it' decided my father, and I was whisked off to Professor Sauerbruch's private clinic. The professor, an eminent surgeon, did not of course bother to attend personally to my insignificant appendix and something went wrong so that I spent six weeks in the clinic with a roaring infection. The wound had to be reopened and packed with gauze, a daily torment to which I did not submit with dignified fortitude. Until the day the deal was made.

I had wanted a bike but had run up against opposition from my parents whose excuse was lack of money. So we struck a deal: I could put 10 marks into my money-box every time I did not yell and struggle when the wound was dressed and the money thus earned would be for the bike. From then on I bit down hard on my thumb during torture time and had 300 marks saved when I came home. As soon as I could walk straight again, I bought my bike: a bright yellow one, with lights and a big bell.

My schooldays in Berlin are a distant blur. There is a photo of me on my first day of school, complete with hat, coat, lunch bag, Waldi, his leash clasped firmly in my left hand, and the traditional big Schultüte or paper bag cradled in my right arm. This was filled with sweets to be shared with my classmates to celebrate my first day in their midst. My mother told me that I refused to go without Waldi.

The only teacher I recall was a fierce Englishwoman who had lived in 'Indiah'. Her skin was leathery, brown and wrinkly, she smelt of cloves and wore tweedy clothes. We had to be perfect in pronunciation. She put her leathery ear close to our mouths and made us repeat: 'Try, try and try again'. The unfortunates who could not roll the English 'r' to her satisfaction were rapped over the knuckles with her ivory ruler. I was lucky enough to be able to roll the 'r's but the 'v's and 'w's give me trouble to this day. I'm not too good on the 'h's before a 'u' either.

Fortunately, my mother was able to retrieve the family albums in the early 1950s.
They are full of photographs of me surrounded with animals of various kinds –
something that still happens today! Fürst, my formidable rabbit, is at bottom right.
Above, I am feeding pigeons in Berlin's Tiergarten, and riding my father's horse Rudi.

Posing with lion cubs at the Berlin zoo.

With Aunt Hannejoh – and another lion, Berlin, 1934

My first day of school, 1935. I refused to go without Waldi.

Formal portrait of Sigrid, Waldi and Helga, Berlin 1938.

Kiwi kids were not the only ones with the freedom to run barefoot. With Sigrid and a Chinese friend.

These wonderful beach chairs provided shelter from the wind and hours of entertainment: tradition demanded that they should be surrounded by elaborately decorated moats.

Playing cowboys and Indians and princesses … and soldiers.

Mutti, Vati and I pose proudly with the new Adler, Berlin 1934.

The villa at Kyllmannstrasse 7, in Berlin, to which we moved in 1937-38. The windows just above ground level mark the location of the cellar where we sheltered during air raids.

CHAPTER 5

War

In the months leading up to the start of the Second World War in September 1939 there had been stories of Polish people ill-treating and even murdering Volksdeutsche (ethnic Germans), who were living in the Polish Corridor, the piece of East Prussia conceded to Poland by the Treaty of Versailles. In my mind I can still see the picture that appeared in a newspaper: it showed the body of a slain woman sprawled on a pavement, her blood running into the gutter. I think the Blitzkrieg against Poland was quite a popular action; the public had been well prepared by the propaganda machine to feel it was time to 'teach the Poles a lesson', to 'protect our people from Polish thugs' and to reclaim our German soil, which had been annexed by Poland after the First World War.

The integration of Austria and the Sudetenland (Boehmen and Mähren-Bohemia and Moravia) into Germany had been so successful – 'Heim ins Reich' (home into the realm) had been the slogans for these campaigns – and surely the lands of East Prussia fell into the same category. Ethnic Germans had the right to live in Grossdeutschland (Great Germany). That the Blitzkrieg against Poland would lead to the Second World War was probably not anticipated. After all, Neville Chamberlain, the British prime minister and Edouard Daladier, his French counterpart, had declared that there would be peace between Great Britain, France and Great Germany. Great Britain had incorporated Scotland, Wales and Ireland into its 'Reich', so Britain could probably relate to Germany's wish to have its population under one roof. France had not made too much fuss when the German Rhineland had been retaken and, anyway, strong fortifications had been built to guard the border between Germany and France: the Maginot Line by the French, the Siegfried Line by the Germans. Both sides thought their fortifications were invincible. Germany's eastern flank had been

secured by the secret non-aggression pact between our government and that of
the Soviet Union. Although this was not known by the general public, it must
have been a decisive factor when planning the invasion of Poland.

Germany's southern neighbours were no problem: Slovakia and Hungary
were friendly and Italy under Mussolini was an Axis partner, as was Japan on
the other side of the world. So the Blitzkrieg was perceived to be just what its
name implied, a short and swift military action like a bolt of lightning, of no
consequence to any other European country except Germany and Poland. The
reason I believe this to be so is that my father, by then a major in the army, was
able to leave for a month's holiday trip to Spain just before the outbreak of the
Second World War.

In the summer of 1939 Helene, my sister Sigrid, Waldi and I spent an idyllic
month at Feldafing on the shores of the Starnberger See just south of Munich.
We stayed in a wooden boathouse in a small clearing between the beech forest
and the bulrushes of the lake. Because our parents were on holiday in Spain,
we could do as we liked, provided we respected Helene's wishes and phobias.
Her greatest fear was thunderstorms and lightning strikes. During the frequent
thunderstorms of this hot summer she shepherded us inside, closed the wooden
shutters of all windows and doors and made us huddle underneath the heavy
dining table.

That part of the ritual we accepted. But why she always hunted up every
metal object she could find, from cutlery, pots and pans to nail files and scis-
sors, bundled the lot into blankets and tablecloths and threw these bundles
out onto the lawn, we could not really understand. She told us convoluted
and scary stories of fireballs jumping in through open windows in search of
metal objects in the house and of hapless residents who were burnt to a cin-
der, because they had not taken the precautions Helene insisted upon. We
squatted in darkness under the table with her, sweating and counting the seconds between lightning and thunderclaps – 23…24…25 – for anxious and
hungry hours. Every second counted equalled a kilometre of distance between
us and the lightning.

We were not allowed to eat during a thunderstorm either, because the fire-
ball would search out the food in our hands. Helene had solved the feeding
problem in an ingenious way: she did not cook at all. The work gang cutting a
road through the forest surrounding our little house had a mobile kitchen so
we ate what they ate: Leberkäs (meatloaf), Knödl (dumplings), potato salad
and Gulasch (spicy stews). Every morning at 11 o'clock we trundled up the hill

to the workers' kitchen and for 3 marks the cook filled the containers in our basket with enough food to last us for lunch and dinner.

We had a small motorboat to go to the village, but after we had got it stuck in the bulrushes while trying to back it out of the boatshed, we preferred to stay put in our little bay, relying on our caretaker, Herr Fabelhaft (Mr Fabulous) to deliver necessities. Mr Fabulous, a bronzed, athletic young man, could fix anything and knew everything. He was our hero. Every evening he paddled his canoe to our jetty, jumped ashore and made sure that all was well with us. One Sunday he came in the morning, which was unusual. Even more unusual, he was shouting something as he paddled closer. We rushed to the jetty. 'War has been declared! You have to pack up immediately to get back to Berlin.'

We continued to live in Berlin during the first year of the war. As a 10-year-old I did not think of the war as life-threatening for us or anybody I knew. When we listened to radio broadcasts, they seemed like an adventure story that told of the battles our brave soldiers had won, of the advances our armies had made into enemy territories. Our side seemed to be invincible.

Whenever there was a bombing raid, we went down to the cellar and had cocoa and biscuits and played Ludo. Sometimes, when a bomb dropped nearby, the board rattled and the coloured counters fell off. 'Whew, that was close,' we would say and Mr Holz would go out to see if our house was burning, which it wasn't, and then he'd shout 'Cooee' and we would all troop up the cellar steps to watch the anti-aircraft fire unstitch the sky.

After an air raid school did not start until 10 o'clock so this was a chance for me and my classmates to collect shrapnel. We did this with great enthusiasm, not only because it could be reused to make bombs to drop on the enemy, thereby helping the fatherland, but also because for 5 kilos of shrapnel you got a Tommy helmet. I was the first of my class to get one but my mother was angry when I arrived home from school wearing it. 'You could have been blown to smithereens picking up shrapnel and that helmet might have come from a poor boy who was killed at Dunkirk,' she said and I was not allowed to go shrapnel hunting again. She also took my helmet away.

During the early stages of the war there was no hint of the devastating destruction Berlin was to suffer later. Sure, there were Verdunkelung (blackout) regulations in force, which meant that streetlights were dimmed before and totally extinguished during an air raid. There were air raid wardens, who checked that no light penetrated the blackout blinds you had to fasten to your windows. All residences had to set up air raid shelters, usually in the cellar, and these had to be equipped with emergency rations of food and water, blankets and comfortable seating, a first aid kit, torches, candles and matches and, of course, fire extinguishers and buckets of sand. Ours also had a radio, a hot-water jug, a cupboard with food and eating utensils, an old wardrobe containing spare clothing and a card table where we could play games to pass the time. At the up and down wail of the air raid siren, we would pick up Waldi and go down to the shelter; at the monotone all clear signal we went back up. An air raid did not seem to be anything to be frightened of, probably because we lived in a suburb far away from strategic targets, such as the industrial areas or the railways that lay in the centre of that sprawling city of more than three million inhabitants.

The raids became more frequent as time went on. One night, when we were sitting in the cellar, playing Ludo, a bomb fell in the far corner of the garden. It shattered most of the windows of the house, dislodged many roof tiles, obliterated the old lilac bush and made an impressive crater. It also shook us up a bit.

CHAPTER 6

Zakopane

During the winter of 1939-1940 my mother, sister and I were in Zakopane, the holiday resort nestled among the majestic snowy peaks of Poland's Tatra mountains. Poland had been defeated and occupied and, although Partisan activities were beginning, my father must have thought it safe enough for my mother, Sigrid, Waldi and me to travel there. I can still visualise the small peasant houses, some painted a very bright blue, the smart hotel complex we stayed at, the souvenir shop, where I bought a multi-coloured wooden snake that wriggled, and, best of all, the sleigh rides.

You were buttoned into sheepskin-lined bags that had a hot stone at the foot end and reached up to your armpits to keep you from freezing solid in the open sleigh. Two little Panje horses, stocky and thick-coated, trotted or cantered in front, jingling their harness bells. The driver, who stood on a low bar in front of the wooden sleigh, was dressed in white: embroidered felt pants, a sheepskin coat, also embroidered, and a fur hat. One driver let me stand beside him on the bar, and take the reins! He cracked the whip and I shouted 'Hooya' and 'Wychta', held onto the reins for dear life and we thundered away. Bits of snow and ice thrown up by the horses' hooves stung my face and he held me steady with his arm that smelt deliciously of horses and sheep and it was total bliss!

Having installed us in a big, comfortable hotel, my father left, planning to rejoin us and take us home 10 days later. It was the sort of hotel where you put your shoes outside your door in the evening and found them again, beautifully polished, the next morning. Hearing a noise outside our door very early one morning, I surprised the shoe-shine man neatly arranging our shoes in a line on the carpet. I said, 'Danke' (thanks) and he said, 'Bitteschön' (my pleasure) and went quickly along the corridor.

I saw the shoe-shine man later that day, from the window of our bathroom. He was down in the yard playing with a lovely black sheep dog. Of course I had to find my way down to the yard to meet the dog! In spite of the language barrier the three of us understood each other and I found out that the dog's name was Rex. At dinner I saved my piece of steak for Rex, wrapped it in the serviette and later, when I was supposed to be in bed reading, sneaked down the back stairs with my gift. Rex was delighted, but the shoe-shine man seemed disconcerted at my visit. I saw that he had a dirty piece of rag bound around his left hand. Little Florence Nightingale sentiments rising strongly, I asked him to show me his hand and was horrified to find that the rag covered a deep gash across the palm from thumb to wrist.

I flew upstairs, retrieved our first aid kit and insisted on cleaning and bandaging the wound properly. The shoe-shine man was very brave and winced only at the sting of the iodine I poured over his hand. He said 'Danke' when he was all bandaged up and I said 'Bitteschön' and we smiled at each other. My mother told me off for sneaking out, but, being a trained nurse herself, she understood my motives. Next morning she sent for the shoe-shine man, rebandaged his hand herself and said I had done a good job. From then on I was allowed to take the dog Rex on our afternoon outings. He got on well with our Waldi as they both liked retrieving sticks.

Just behind the hotel was the valley terminal of the gondola that took you to the top of a mountain where you could sun-bathe on deckchairs or sit in a restaurant, drink cocoa and admire the view and the skiers swishing down the adjacent piste. Why my mother, sister and I went up there on that afternoon and how we got to the mountain top I cannot recall. But I do remember vividly what happened then and how our holiday came to an abrupt end.

I know we had left Waldi in our room at the hotel, because the snow was too deep for his short legs, but that Rex was with us and that it had started to snow again – and how afraid we were. We had reached the restaurant and found the door locked. No lights, no activity inside, no answer to our knocking. 'We'll take the next gondola down,' said my mother, taking us firmly by the hand and marching us to the terminal. It, too, was bolted shut and there was nobody around to reply to our calls. 'We'll walk down the short cut,' whispered my mother and the tight grip on my hand transmitted her feeling of urgency and unease. The short cut was a steep zigzag path through the dark fir trees that flanked the line of pylons for the gondola. We started down, very quickly, too quickly for my little sister, who kept stumbling. The snow came down quickly too and got heavier. Dusk was falling. Branches were snapping. making cracking sounds. Nobody was there, except us three and Rex. There were wolves in these mountains, and rabies was rife.

It was no use calling for help, no one would hear us and no one would want to help us! I remembered my father saying, 'Be careful. Polish people have no reason to like us.' Rex, straining at his leash, was making little whining sounds, as was Sigrid. My mother held onto her, firmly, while Rex and I stumbled behind. It was a long way down yet. Faster and faster we went, with branches cracking all around us now, when we heard a shot and a muffled scream. There was more rifle fire in the distance to our left. Panic-stricken, we started to run. Suddenly, ahead of us, a dark shape disengaged itself from a tree trunk. There was the gleam of a gun barrel. We stopped and stood dead still, except Rex who was barking and howling and jumping around. I could hardly hold him. The shape came nearer and the voice was an urgent hiss: 'Is all right. Friend. Go. I follow.' It was the shoe-shine man.

We quickly and quietly walked the rest of the zigzag, the shoe-shine man a few paces behind us, rifle in the crook of his arm. He vanished just before we reached the circle of lights at the back of the hotel. In the lobby we were met by my father's aide-de-camp who, tight-lipped, informed us that we were to leave with him this minute: my father was waiting for us at Krakow. Our luggage would follow. I just had time to bend down and cuddle Rex, surreptitiously entwining my gold-chain necklace around his collar, before we were bundled into the car. We left with an armed escort.

Although it was a secret, I found out that the 'Zakopane incident', where several soldiers and civilians had been killed, was part of a Partisan campaign. The Partisans were an underground movement of Polish freedom fighters who harassed and sabotaged the German occupying force whenever and wherever an opportunity arose.

I fully expected to be reprimanded when it was discovered that my gold chain was missing. Fashioned from part of my grandfather's watch chain, it had been a birthday present from my grandmother. My mother asked me if I had any idea of where it could be. When I answered, 'Yes, it's around Rex's neck', she just looked at me and then hugged me, her eyes brimming.

The Zakopane incident was never talked about again in our family, but soon after my mother gave me a bracelet, made from the same watch chain. I have it still.

39

CHAPTER 7

Garmisch

M y father decided that it was no longer safe for his family in Berlin and in the spring of 1941 moved us south into the mountains of Bavaria, to Garmisch, where we lived with our Aunt Erna. She owned a Saluki hound called Sascha who mindlessly chased everything that moved at speed. He raced alongside trains and was faster than most cars. 'He's as crazy as she is' was my father's uncharitable comment about his cousin and Sascha.

He did have a point, though – Aunt Erna did have peculiar habits. She appeared relatively normal until after lunch. Then she changed into a colourful silk gown, set her drawing room table with a lace cloth, floral arrangements, her best tea set and the silver samovar, drew the curtains and waited for her visitor. 'I'm expecting the Emperor of China to call,' she announced through a crack in the door. 'Please inform me of his arrival and be sure you show His Majesty due respect.' We would have too, but, sad to say, the Emperor of China never did come for afternoon tea, although Aunt Erna prepared for his arrival every day. I supposed he had more pressing matters to attend to at home, what with Chiang Kai-shek and Manchuria, Mao Tse Tung and all the other unpleasant happenings in his empire.

Many families had relocated to the safety of Garmisch. The Lyceum (high school for girls) had closed its roll and so I had to attend the Gymnasium (high school for boys) run by Jesuit fathers. They were not keen to have a girl in their all-male establishment and made this very clear. 'She will have to take Latin and keep to our curriculum.' This was meant as a deterrent, but my parents persisted. At the age of eleven I wore braces on my teeth and resembled a solid barrel with roughly the same measurements for chest and waist. In my mind all boys were ghastly and I'm sure they felt the same about me. They let down the tyres of my yellow bike, they stole my coloured pencils, they called me rude names. In class I shared a desk with a particularly obnoxious boy who never did his Latin homework. I did mine because I liked Latin. He used to copy off me and whenever I objected to this he pinched me, hard, so that I had big bruises on my left thigh. But one day I got him. The classroom had been deathly quiet, with Father dozing at his desk. We were writing a Latin test and the obnoxious boy wanted to copy off my paper. He pinched again so I grabbed his hand and bit it, hard, drawing blood.

He yelped. Father, startled into wakefulness, approached, much displeased. 'She bit me!' the boy whinged, holding up his injured hand. 'He pinched me!' I shouted and displayed my bruised thigh. The class rioted joyously, Father swept out of the room and returned with Monsignor. Decorum was restored, the boy was punished, but I was not even reprimanded. Perhaps Monsignor saw that justice had been done, perhaps he was secretly amused, or perhaps he was not equipped to cope with a biting female who exposed a thigh. Anyway not only did the pinching cease, but I had won the respect of my classmates and was treated as 'one of the boys' from then on.

I am fond of Latin to this day; it helps with spelling. Casually inserting a Latin quote into a conversation has good snob value too. It does not matter greatly whether the quote is relevant to the situation; a 'navigare necesse est' or 'scientia potestas est', murmured with a sage nod of the head, is usually well received. Not many people are fluent in Latin nowadays.

When a place at the Lyceum became available and I was shifted to this genteel establishment run by nuns, I was reluctant to leave my mates and adjust to femininity again. Proud of their highly polished floors, the nuns made us wear slippers inside the school building. That was all right: you could run and then slide along corridors at breakneck speed, if the nuns weren't watching. They also made us wear gingham pinafores and checked for clean hankies and clean fingernails every morning. That took a bit of getting used to. Apart from requiring me to be tidy, clean and polite, the Lyceum presented no great challenges that I remember. During the years of my primary and secondary education I attended eight schools. Not because I was kicked out of seven, as I always pointed out to my pupils when, much later in life I had become a teacher, but because my family moved to different places during my school years. My education was somewhat patchy as a result. In geography I studied North America three times and missed out on Asia altogether. I am well versed in long division and multiplication tables, but the esoterica of square roots and the mysteries of Pythagoras elude me to this day.

Behind us in a smallish wooden chalet lived 'the American'. An elderly gentleman, rosy, rotund, clean-shaven and always adorned with a bow-tie, he smoked a delicious-smelling tobacco in his pipe and was glad of the company my friends and I provided. We seemed to be the only visitors who interrupted his writing and broadcasting. 'Howdy,' he would smile through the window when we waved to be let in. His door was always locked and he scrabbled around mysteriously inside before opening it. He had a microphone, headphones and several black boxes with dials on his desk, which was piled high with lots of folders and sheaves of typing paper.

He adored the wild strawberries we picked for him and fed us 'candy' in return. Amused when we attempted to converse with him in schoolgirl English, he taught us some more or less respectable American slang words, such as 'kid', 'buster' and 'okay'. I now suspect that he was engaged either in broadcasting propaganda or decoding secret messages. Probably an outcast from his own country, he lived a lonely existence among strangers. Did he have strong convictions that led to his clandestine activities or did he do it for money? Was he a spy? A double agent? What became of him? Whoever or whatever he was, he was a kindly grandfatherly figure during our time in Garmisch.

We did not know our other neighbours very well. The old military gentleman across the road insisted on being addressed as 'Your Excellency'. A relic of the monarchy, he strode about, ramrod straight, swinging a silver-topped walking stick in a menacing sort of way. His name was von Zigesar but his straggly beard made him look a bit like a goat buck (Ziegenbock) so we called him 'His Excellency von Ziegenbart' (goat beard). On the south side lived the composer Richard Strauss who worked away locked behind a high wrought iron gate, emerging only occasionally to complain about our Waldi, whose bark must have introduced a jarring dissonance into Mr Strauss's tonal compositions.

My father did not stay with us in Garmisch. He was away 'at the war' and came for a few days only every now and then. These times were always special. My mother glowed and he made time to play games with my sister and have serious talks with me. His career had moved in a new direction by this time. He was no longer in the army, but was now second in command of the NSKK, the National Sozialistisches Kraftfahr Korps (National Socialist Vehicle Corps). This, presumably, was a desk job at HQ; he would rather have been in active service at the front.

The war had expanded enormously. German troops and their allies were now fighting simultaneously on many fronts, in North Africa, Greece, the Balkans and in the Soviet Union. Although most of the German campaigns were still successful, Rudolf Hess, Hitler's deputy, must have seen the writing on the wall. In May 1941, on the eve of Germany's attack on Russia, he flew secretly to Scotland in an attempt to negotiate a peace agreement with the Western allies. Strange as it may seem, Britain and the United States were not perceived to be arch enemies, in spite of mutual bombing raids. A spirit of chivalry prevailed in the North African campaign and the battles at sea were also fought with both sides adhering to a code of honour.

The fight against the communists was a fight against the arch enemy; the war in the Soviet Union was fought with no quarter given, and atrocities committed by both sides. It was a clash of ideologies. Communism saw itself as reshaping world order, destroying the class system, destroying religion, destroying national identity in the process of achieving its goal of the rule of the proletariat, a classless international society. National Socialism saw itself as the bulwark against the 'Reds', safeguarding not only German national identity, but the cultural heritage of Western civilisation. National Socialism and communism in fact had many aspects in common. Both were committed to bettering the living conditions of their respective peoples, both were authoritarian regimes, both demanded unquestioning loyalty to their leaders and both pursued their respective ideologies with a religious fervour that allowed no room for mercy, tolerance or pragmatic thinking.

In Garmisch, where no bombing raids occurred, the progress of the war was not an issue that occupied much of my 12-year-old thinking, but I remember seeing the columns of young men of the Gebirgsjäger (mountain hunter) units marching past to and from their barracks. They sang as they marched: 'Auf dem Berg da blüht ein kleines Blümelein und das heisst Edelweiss' (on the mountain blooms a small flower, called Edelweiss). Beautiful young men they were, so bronzed, healthy and happy. I watched them with pride. They were soon sent off to the Russian front where many of them perished in the cruel winter campaigns and during the siege of Leningrad.

Within a few months I changed from a barrel-shaped kid with pigtails into a long-legged teenager who grew her hair to shoulder length and even put in curlers at night. Boys were not an issue yet but my dearest girlfriend Gerda and I had deep discussions about babies and such. Her mother, like mine, seemed to be unapproachable on these delicate matters, so we shared the misinformation gathered from classmates. Gerda and I have remained close friends to this day. We are both grandmothers now and, as she and I managed to produce three children each, it can be deduced that we have acquired the relevant information about babies and suchlike during the past 50 years.

Finding the first blue gentian flowers and wild primulas in the spring, picking tiny wood strawberries and swimming in the Rissersee in the summer, skating and skiing in the winter, riding the cable cars up to the Kreuzeck to run all the way down the mountains on the zigzag paths, taking Waldi and crazy Sascha for long walks through the adjoining meadows and woods, all these carefree activities came to an end when we moved to Munich.

CHAPTER 8

Munich

I was sad to leave Gerda, the American and my school friends when we shifted to Munich. We moved into a large apartment in Wiedemayer Strasse and for the first time I had my own room. That was nice, and I also liked the lift that took us up to our third floor, but I missed the mountains and the freedom we had in Garmisch. I guess the reason for the move was related to my father's career, although he was not often home with us at all. We settled in and I was enrolled at St Anna's, a very conservative Catholic girls' school, which was not to my liking.

In the autumn of 1942 the air raids became more serious. A total blackout was imposed: no light was allowed to escape from any window and we drew heavy blackout curtains every evening. Two or three times a week we had to go down to the communal bomb shelter, which was set up in the supposedly safest area, in the middle of the building's basement. It was equipped with wooden benches around the walls, there was a first aid kit, a fire extinguisher, a water tap and many buckets of sand and shovels.

I learned to be tidy because it was essential for the routine of getting quickly to the shelter when the alarm sounded. Your shoes had to sit next to the bed, side by side, toes pointing out, laces undone, socks laid on top, so that you could jump into them when half asleep. Your clothes had to be on a chair with underwear on top of the pile, and you kept a torch under your pillow. We each had a small suitcase of spare clothing and a box of foodstuffs permanently in our cellar, an enclosed storeroom that went with the apartment.

Waldi's spare basket was also in this storeroom; he was incarcerated there during air raids as dogs were verboten (forbidden) to come into the human shelter. Waldi had to wear his collar and leash to bed, so that he could be grabbed quickly and galloped down the back stairs. We could not use the lift in case of power failure. This was not fun any more; we did not play Ludo down in this cellar.

Not all the occupants of the house went to the shelter, some preferring to stay in their apartments. The family who lived above us came down. Their son Helmut and I first exchanged smiles while sitting on our wooden benches, smiles that later led to our platonic romance. The family who lived below us came too: several small whiny children, a harassed and downtrodden mother and their father, a thin man with little black eyes whom we called the 'Goldfasan' (golden pheasant) because he strutted about in the gold-brown uniform of a party official, organising everybody into places and rosters for fire duty. Mr and Mrs Mothwurf, the elderly Jewish couple who lived on the first floor, were usually the first to arrive in the shelter. They sat hand in hand in the far corner and spoke only in whispers, mostly to each other. There was not much talk among the residents anyway as we all sat quietly and listened worriedly for the whine of the bombs.

If you heard them whine, they landed somewhere else; a direct hit was not preceded by a whine, we had been told. The planes dropped a lot of incendiary bombs too. Black, hollow sticks about 50 centimetres long, containing phosphorus, they fizzed for a minute or two before they exploded, spraying their contents and setting everything alight. Whenever there was a pause in the ack-ack-ack of anti-aircraft fire and the whine and detonations of bombs, we used to rush the six floors up to the attic to check if any of these Brandbomben (fire bombs) had dropped through the roof. If you were quick enough and grabbed the non-fizzing end, you could hurl the thing out of an attic window down into the garden, where it exploded more or less harmlessly. One day Helene, our intrepid housekeeper, got hold of one that was fizzing rather menacingly already. Panic-stricken, she ran around with it in her hand. 'Throw it down!' we yelled, equally terrified. Opening the iron door of the central heating flue, she threw the bomb down so that it landed in the furnace in the cellar and exploded there. The whole house was without heating for a week and Helene was not popular.

The worst night in the shelter was when the house next door scored a hit and the rubble blocked the exit from our shelter. We sat for hours, mostly in darkness, because there was no power and we wanted to save our torch batteries. We listened to the drip drip drip of a broken water pipe and hoped the gas pipes had remained intact. We knew we were going to be rescued eventually, but we were afraid. It was very dark and oppressive and quiet, apart from occasional sniffling from the gold pheasant's infants. Suddenly his voice rang out: 'Before we all suffocate down here, I'm going to shoot the Jews. It's their friends who drop the bombs on us!' Mr and Mrs Mothwurf did not say a word. Neither did the rest of us. We were all shocked by this sudden outburst. He did not shoot them and we were dug out from the rubble shortly afterwards, but the Mothwurfs never used the shelter again. They set up chairs and a table in their own storeroom and camped there, just like Waldi.

The war droned on. We had got used to ration cards, which gave every person an allocation of food and clothing coupons. Although we could not buy everything we wanted – I cannot recall ever eating bananas or oranges during those years – there was no shortage of basic food or clothing until the very last days of the war. We had got used to the air raid sirens and the bombing raids, which at that time occurred mostly during the night. Going down to the bomb shelter in our cellar had almost become a routine. It was only sometimes, when the bombs fell a bit too close, that we were scared.

Every evening we listened to the news bulletins from various battlefields. Sometimes the news was good: a battle had been won, an advance had been made. But sometimes the news was bad and if that was the case, one did not talk about it. At that stage, no one in my immediate family had suffered personally as a result of the war. It was still waged outside the borders of Germany, and the dying and devastation were too far away to affect my day-to-day thoughts. I knew at this time that there was a concentration camp at Dachau, not far from Munich, and that 'traitors' and Jews were sent there, but I honestly thought they were taken there to learn to concentrate on positive thoughts, to see the light, as it were. I knew nothing about the atrocities perpetrated there. Traitors and concentration camps and defeat at the fronts were taboo subjects anyway. To talk about them would have been disloyal to my father and also to the Führer, to whom we had sworn allegiance. It would have been dangerous for anyone else to voice 'treacherous' opinions to me: I might have prattled about them to others.

CHAPTER 9

Erika

The move from Garmisch to Munich was for me, I think, also the move
from childhood to adolescence. Life was not as straightforward as it used
to be; new feelings and perceptions developed and deepened. Erika Hirsch
was probably the catalyst for many of these. She became my best friend in
Munich. We went to the same school and neither of us fitted well into the
docile young lady image St Anna's required. This was a common bond: we
liked each other instantly and became staunch friends in spite of our different
backgrounds.

Erika, of slight build, with sparkling blue eyes and a cheerful round face
topped by short blonde bangs, was much more worldly-wise than I. Her training as ballet dancer in the junior class of the Munich State Opera opened a
vista far removed from St Anna's to her and, by association, to me. When she
went to the opera for rehearsals, I often tagged along into that magic realm of
the stage behind the curtain. As long as I stood unobtrusively in a corner, I
became part of the backdrop. The corps de ballet, singers, stage-hands and
principals flowed past, oblivious of my existence. Transfixed by the intoxicat-
ing atmosphere, I watched and listened to the shouting, singing, panting,
running, leaping of the chorus and ballet, the cacophony of the orchestra tun-
ing up, the scenery being shifted by burly stage-hands, the backdrops moving
up or down by clanking chains. Lights now blazing, now dimmed, the smell
of greasepaint, sweat and dust. My heart pounded.

It pounded even harder when my favourite tenor, Franz Klarwein, made an
appearance. I adored him. Before Erika let me come to rehearsals with her, I
had worshipped him from a distance only, having gone to every production
he starred in. Although he looked and bowed in the direction of our box in
response to my fervent clapping, I knew that he was not aware of me in par-

ticular, that the look and bow were part of the etiquette of acknowledging applause. The shadowy figure of an adolescent girl in her best blue velvet frock clapping so hard that her hands hurt made no impact on him. It did not matter that he was still unaware of me when, thanks to Erika, I got much closer to my idol. One day when I was lurking in the shadow of the wings he came so close that he almost tripped over me. Although the glance he bestowed on me with his beautiful dark eyes was less than loving, I nearly fainted with delight.

We often went to the opera during our time in Munich. An ardent music lover, my father had leased a box for us, the Proscenium Loge, two tiers up on the left side of the orchestra. Whenever he was home, we went to the opera together and took the orchestra score with us. He followed the music avidly, balancing the heavy leather-bound volume on the balustrade of the box. I will never forget the night when this got us into trouble. Wagner's *Die Meistersinger* is a lengthy opera and the conductor had shortened the score by omitting a phrase or two here and there. This meant we had to flip the pages of our score over at furious speed to keep pace. We flipped too vigorously. The book sailed down into the orchestra pit, on top of the Flügelhorns, who were not pleased. My father had to apologise profusely and shout them a case of champagne.

We were growing up. Erika had a real boyfriend already. I never met him, but she told me about their mind-boggling activities. I, on the other hand, had three love affairs proceeding simultaneously, even if they were all platonic.

Franz Klarwein, the tenor, still featured as number one in my dreams. My second love affair was multiple.

I could not make up my mind who of the five young men we called 'the Bulgarian Spies' was the most desirable. They gave the impression of coming from the Balkans. They lived on the fifth floor of our apartment block which meant they used the lift when coming and going to their secret and dangerous assignments. Erika and I took to hanging about in the foyer, waiting to get into the lift with them. We rode up to the fifth floor in their company; to get out on the third floor, where my family lived, seemed hardly worthwhile. They were always courteous, letting us enter and leave first, but they never spoke to us, not even to say 'Please, after you', or suchlike. All five were tall, dark and handsome, one with a pencil-thin moustache gracing his upper lip, one with a well-trimmed black goatee beard. They favoured trench coats or, in inclement weather, long dark overcoats, as befitted spies. So mysterious, so nefarious, so spy-like delicious – Erika and I made up lots of romantic and heroic stories about them. I was quite devastated when they suddenly disappeared without a trace. One day in the lift, the next day gone, their dangerous mission completed, no doubt.

My third love affair failed to impress Erika. She just snorted derisively whenever I mentioned Helmut, whom I had met in the communal bomb shelter. He was 13 already, red-haired, freckle-faced, knobbly-kneed and very clever. His bedroom was directly above mine which was handy, because he taught me Morse code and rigged up sending and receiving devices in both our rooms, with the wire running from his window to mine, so we could converse at night. We started off with great enthusiasm, but found it hard to keep the momentum going. Tapping out meaningful messages with the correct long and short dot and dash for every letter was a rather long-winded process for an impatient person like me. Helmut got cross when I did not speedily decode his dots and sent garbled replies. When he suggested that we should tap out a story to each other for practice, such as Little Red Riding Hood, I could understand why Erika had snorted. End of affair. I gave him back his Morse code device and he dismantled the wire. He was probably as relieved as I was to end our electronic relationship.

Erika and I met Hitler one afternoon, quite by chance.

We were ambling home from school, the long way, past the building of the Airforce Ministry. Official-looking cars were parked at the kerb, there were guards at the entrance and quite a few people stood around waiting. When we asked what was happening, we were told 'The Führer is inside. He's coming out soon.' I became very excited: our leader – and we were about to see him, up close!

Erika, although a trifle less enthusiastic than I, nevertheless loyally helped me to pick some flowering forsythia branches from a nearby hedge. We wriggled through the spectators to stand right beside the steps. When he came out in a group of officers I shouted 'Sieg Heil!' and waved the forsythia. He smiled and walked over to us, asked our names, accepted the flowers, told us we were good girls and shook our hands. He still had the bright blue charismatic eyes I remembered from the day of the parade in Berlin, and his personality had the same compelling effect on me. He was the Führer, the leader, whom I would follow and obey without question. If he had asked me to lay down my life for him that minute, I would still have died on the spot, without hesitation.

'I'll never wash my right hand again, this hand the Führer touched!' I vowed when I got home. 'In that case you'll not sit at the dinner table,' retorted my mother. 'Remember, it's what's inside you that counts, not what's on the out-side.' I washed my hands but inside I was elated for days.

Reflecting on this incident now several facts strike me. Erika's father was Jewish. She may have been the only non-Aryan girl ever to shake hands with and be complimented by Hitler. The reason for her lack of enthusiasm never occurred to me at the time. My own fervour stemmed from being brainwashed into thinking that Hitler was a Messiah-like figure who could do no wrong. He was to be looked up to, he was to be obeyed. He led, we followed. It took a lot of soul-searching, rejecting and revising of ideas after the end of the Third Reich for me to formulate a different philosophy of life from the Weltan-schauung (world view) I had grown up with.

Erika lived in the same street, just a few houses along, near the pub at the corner. Her house did not have a lift; you had to climb the stairs up to the fifth floor where she lived. Her mother was a thin, anxious woman, disfigured by a scar that ran from the cheekbone to the left corner of her mouth. I do not remember her ever wearing anything else but a floral wrap-around apron. Erika was her only child and she fussed over her in a loving and ineffectual way. Erika treated her mother with affectionate contempt and did pretty well as she liked.

Herr Hirsch lived unobtrusively in the back room of their flat, smoking cigars, listening to the radio and playing chess against himself all day long. A rotund, red-faced man with an untidy halo of sparse grey hair and stubbly jowls, he had twinkly, kindly eyes and was jolly and friendly. 'How's the war going, girlie?' he always asked me when I came to visit and I always replied, 'Very well, thank you', at which he chortled. Often he asked Erika and me to run down to the pub to buy him cigars and some bottles of beer. 'Not healthy for me to be about the street too much in the light of day,' he chuckled, spreading his hands and hooking his thumbs under his braces.

Poor Mr Hirsch, he must have been bored and lonely, cooped up in that back room. I would like to be able to report that he lived a happy and fulfilled life after the collapse of Nazism, but, sadly, he died of a heart attack a few weeks before the end of the war. Erika's house was hit during a bombing raid. A bomb tore out the front part of the family's dining room, leaving a gaping hole where the table had stood. You could look from the door frame of the hall right down to the crater in the front garden. Mr Hirsch had stayed in his back room when the bomb fell and he must have come out when the dust had settled. Confronted by the big hole where his dining table had been, he collapsed and died. Erika and her mother found him lying in the hall when they came up from the bomb shelter.

I heard about this tragedy only during the winter of 1945-1946, when I renewed my friendship with Erika. We had lost contact after my family moved from Munich in 1943, neither of us being good correspondents. Erika and her mother still lived in the ruins of their apartment. They had simply nailed a few boards across the gaping hole and hung a curtain from the door frame to keep out the cold draughts. Of course the house was condemned as unsafe and they were staying there illegally, but they had not found anywhere else to live.

I had gone to their place seeking shelter for the night, having missed the evening train south to Kreuth, where we lived at that time. Erika's mother made me very welcome. She shared her pot of soup with me and told me about her husband and daughter. Erika was not dancing any more. The opera had also suffered a direct hit so there were no performances, no corps de ballet now. But Erika was fine, she was going out a lot and had many friends. Erika had not returned home by the time I left early the next morning.

When I called again a few months later, Erika was home and we were delighted to see each other again. She did look fine and sophisticated and, in contrast to me, was most fashionably dressed, even down to her nylon stockings. 'Stay the night and come to a party with me,' she urged. 'It will be fun.' And so I went. At the party there were a lot of people of different nationalities, a sprinkling of American servicemen and only a few Germans, mostly girls, and more food and drink than I had seen for many a day. The music was loud and everybody was very jolly and huggy and kissy but I felt uneasy, out of place and gauche. Erika had waltzed off in the arms of a swarthy-looking man and was nowhere to be found. When an inebriated individual wrapped his arms around me and breathed, 'Come along, girl, what's your name?', I wriggled free with some force and ran, having realised that a fate worse than death was about to engulf me.

There must have been some repercussions, because Erika was furious with me when she returned home the next morning. We had words and parted on a cool note. When I saw Erika again many months later, however, she was full of fun, bubbling with happiness and generous as usual. She offered me six Hershey chocolate bars. She had a whole box of them, she told me, from one of her American GI boyfriends. 'These guys are the best,' she said. She was going to get one to marry her and then she would live in the States, in clover. She wanted me to go to another party with her, a 'fishing party' she called it, but I declined, suspecting that her ideas and mine about fishing parties might be different.

I never saw Erika again. When I next came to Munich and looked for her house, it had been demolished. The new owners of the corner pub had no idea who Erika was and where she and her mother might be. I hope Erika made it to the States and is living there, happily and in clover. Fun-loving, warm-hearted and generous, my friend Erika deserves the best.

CHAPTER 10

Bad Harzburg

Early in 1943, I cannot remember the exact date, we moved from Munich to Bad Harzburg, a pretty little spa situated at the north end of the Harz Mountains, about an hour's drive south from Braunschweig. Although it suffered very little damage during the Second World War, it fell upon hard times in 1945 when the town was occupied by first the British, then the Russian forces, then by the British again. When the border between East and West Germany was finally established, the Iron Curtain ran through the fields and hills just 3 kilometres east of the town. The double line of electrified high wire fences, interspersed with watch towers, and an expanse of bare earth known as the Todes Streifen (death strip), was very visible, very menacing and very close.

The house we had lived in served as living quarters for officers of the British forces and most of its contents were souvenired as war booty by these gentlemen. Years later when my mother was allowed to retrieve the few pieces of furniture that had been too heavy to remove, she found deep gouges in the top of her antique writing desk that spelled out the name of a British colonel and that somebody had carved 'Kilroy was here' into the lid of the grand piano.

The move to Bad Harzburg was related to my father's new position. He had been disappointed not to get promoted to head of the NSKK when the previous chief died. It was then that Himmler approached him again with the offer to join the SS, with promotion to General der Waffen SS (the military side of the SS), Obergruppenführer and Chief of Police, responsible for Abschnitt Mitte (the middle section of Germany). This time my father accepted. I know that my mother was not happy about the decision and I think my father had misgivings too, but Himmler had promised active service at the front in the near future, which may have been the deciding factor. I overheard a conversation between my parents, when my father said, 'I told him I will not have anything to do with the Jewish problem.' He did not, either, to the best of my knowledge.

But he knew. They all knew. Nobody talked about it. Those who perpetrated the horrors in the concentration camps kept quiet. Were they ashamed? Those who were potential victims kept quiet too, because they were afraid. The few Jewish people I had met kept a low profile. I did not think of them as enemies. Mr Hirsch, the father of my best friend Erika, was a very jovial gentleman and Mr and Mrs Mothwurf, who lived in the same house as my family in Munich, were a pleasant old couple.

It seems strange now that, on a personal level, I did not think of the Jewish people I knew as 'Jews', or as bad or a threat or even different, but I had certainly absorbed my share of the ideology of anti-Semitism and propaganda from school and from the BDM (the Bund Deutscher Mädchen or Federation of German Girls), which I had just joined. I was taught that the Jews, as a collective and alien entity, were to blame for the misery of the Depression years, that they had manipulated the economy and profited when German people were starving and that all through history they had been troublemakers: they had never assimilated into the countries they lived in and, not least of all, they had been responsible for killing Christ.

'The Jews killed Jesus' was a propaganda slogan widely accepted by people who conveniently forgot that Christ himself was a Jew. One might as well have blamed the Italians, because Pontius Pilate, the Roman Governor of Judea, ordered the execution of Jesus. But that would not have been politically expedient; the Italians under Mussolini were our allies. And that anti-Semitic slogan was not an invention of Joseph Goebbels' fertile brain; it had been one of the catalysts for pogroms against the Jewish population in Christian countries for centuries before the advent of Hitler. Portraying the Jews as the Antichrist, therefore foes of the Christian church, may be one of the reasons why there was no public outcry against their persecution.

There was also that nonsense about being of the Aryan race and keeping your blood pure. People in the army or public service had to be in possession of an Ahnenpass, a document proving that their ancestry had not been contaminated by Jewish blood in centuries past. Mine, which had been researched through church records back to the 17th century, showed all sorts of interesting people in my lineage, including a shepherd, an ivory carver, many peasants, some merchants and a vague connection to royalty, but no 'contamination'. I wonder what would have happened to my father's career if a Jewish ancestor had popped out of the woodwork.

Propaganda is a very powerful and mind-bending tool, which those in power have employed successfully throughout history. The Jews, like the communists, were portrayed by the media as symbols of darkness and evil against which our valiant heroes fought bravely to preserve the integrity and culture of the fatherland and ensure its glorious future. A bit like St George and the dragon. I've since revised my thoughts about him too, along with my ideas about anti-Semitism, communism, nationalism, fascism, racism, materialism and the various -isms of religion.

The big house we rented in Bad Harzburg stood in park-like grounds. The owner, a widow and her crippled daughter, lived in the gate house. Her poor husband had shot himself, having been involved in some scandal. His mother had died in the house many years ago and the urn containing her ashes sat high up in a fork of the branches of an enormous elm tree in the grounds. The main entrance had big wrought iron gates set into stone pillars which were surmounted by a gable adorned with a relief sculpture of a monkey and a golden 'Z', like the entrance to a zoo.

The monkey had an evil grin and staring eyes. I was never comfortable when I had to use this gate and I kept well away from the elm tree too. There are some houses that emanate ill fortune and I believe this was one of them. Others must have felt it too. Long after the turbulent times when its original owners, as well as my family and the various military occupiers of the post-war period, had departed, every room of the house was exorcised by a priest on request of the new owner.

The house had three storeys. On the ground floor was a big hall, which we used as a lounge. Downstairs were also my father's study, my mother's drawing room and the dining room, connected by a passage to the kitchen. On the first floor was a hall with a billiards table and a gallery that led into the two bathrooms and my parents' bedroom. My sister's and my bedrooms were on the other side of the hall, separated by the stairs that led up to the attic rooms, Helene's self-contained apartment. The place was certainly too big for Helene to keep tidy, so there were 'dailies' who did the cleaning, washing and ironing, and a gardener.

We should have been comfortable, we should have been happy there as a family, but we were not. My father was away a lot and when he was at home, he no longer had the time to talk with me about my problems; he probably had enough of his own. My mother had started to nurse the wounded soldiers in the Harzburger Hof, the hotel across the road which had been converted into a military hospital. When she came home she was exhausted and not at all inclined to listen to my small concerns either.

Just before my 14th birthday, I decided it was time that I, too, made a contribution to the war effort. My first attempt was to work, unpaid and unskilled, in a lemonade plant, replacing an adult who could then do a more important job. So I was told, when I reported on the first day of the school holidays. I had to check that the bottles, which coasted past me at a fast clip, had been filled to the top. If one wasn't, I had to grab it quickly and put it into a wire mesh basket. I had to wear gumboots and a long rubber apron, but I got wet and sticky all the same. After a month of this, I clumsily grabbed a broken bottle and cut my little finger to the bone. 'That's the end of it!' stormed my father and I was secretly relieved. Working in the lemonade plant had been rather boring.

My next war effort was to help in the hospital where my mother worked, every weekday after school except Wednesdays when I attended the BDM meetings. At first a group of us had the job of rolling bandages and folding linen. Then we were promoted to 'bringing cheer to the patients', which involved helping to feed those who could not feed themselves, running messages, arranging flowers and taking those who could walk on crutches or who were in wheelchairs for outings to the Kurpark surrounding the hospital.

I was chuffed when I was asked to help with theatre duties because I could wear a blue protective gown, even if my duties meant only that I scrubbed the basins and mopped the floor. One day I had to take a big, lidded, stainless steel bucket down to the incinerator. I had not been told that it contained an amputated foot. When I was skipping downstairs, swinging the bucket, the lid fell off and the bluishly gruesome foot tumbled out. Abandoning bucket and foot, I fled upstairs and was violently sick in the corridor.

'No more,' said my mother, signalling the end of my volunteer war efforts in the hospital theatre. This was just as well, because towards the end of 1943 and throughout the next year the war efforts I was called upon to do took all my spare time and energy anyway, with school playing a secondary role. The only nice thing about school was the new friendships I gained, particularly my close friendship with Inge. We had much in common. Her father was a prominent person too and, like me, she had boyfriend troubles at the time. Our friendship lasted and grew stronger and Inge remained my faithful and help-ful friend and confidante all her life, although we only saw each other a few times after I had emigrated to New Zealand. She died four years ago and I miss her.

I did not like school any more; most lessons seemed irrelevant to what was really happening around me. My worst subject was still mathematics and avoid-ing tests became a challenge. The most successful way of doing this was courtesy of the daily fly-over by bombing squadrons. Everybody was nervous about these air raids and the school rule was that we all dived into the bomb shelter for cover at the first sound of planes approaching. The sirens did not always give early warning so, with a maths test looming, I would suddenly sit up startled and straight and call out, 'I can hear planes!', at which my classmates, who had been waiting for this signal, and I would stampede into the shelter. It worked nearly every time, even if we had to wait for a while until the planes really did drone overhead.

There was no bomb damage in Bad Harzburg itself while we lived there; the squadrons flew over us to bomb the Ruhr cities and the hydro dams. In the later stages of the war the boys in the school who were older than 15 were drafted to man the anti-aircraft guns stationed at these dams. They did so on a roster system: for three days they were schoolboys, for three days they were soldiers. When the 'Dam Busters' dropped the rolling bomb and destroyed the Möhne Dam, four of my schoolmates were killed.

Every so often we were given a few hours off school to collect Stanniol Streifen, tin foil strips that were dropped in quantity by Allied planes to pre-vent detection by German radar. There were usually propaganda leaflets among the silver paper too, bearing messages like 'Surrender to avoid total destruc-tion' and 'Get rid of Hitler and his henchmen before it is too late'.

We were issued with big brown paper sacks and taken to the surrounding countryside in army trucks to scrounge around for strips and leaflets. This was fun. It was not so funny when the army trucks collected us from school one morning to help clean up a nearby village that had been totally destroyed the night before when the bombers had been intercepted and dropped their load to facilitate a fast retreat. By the time we got there, the dead and dying had been removed and we had to help the survivors to salvage a few possessions and clear the rubble as best we could. The boys were given shovels; we girls were issued with gloves that were far too big for us. I helped an old lady search for her goat. We found it, squashed dead under the collapsed roof of a shed, a little white goat with a collar and a bell around its neck. The old lady cried and I cried with her.

As the bombing increased, so did the casualties. Some of the people killed, soldiers and civilians, had a Staatsbegräbnis (state funeral). Along with my classmates I donned my BDM uniform of white shirt with insignia, black scarf with a brown leather toggle, black skirt, white socks and black shoes, to form the guard of honour. Two lines of girls, heads bowed, stood absolutely still in the aisle of the Kurhalle (spa complex) where the services took place and two girls flanked the coffin on the stage. Because we were tall, I guess, my best friend Inge and I often had to be the ones flanking the coffin and later carrying the official wreath. It was hard standing still and looking solemn for ages, while facing the congregation.

On one terrible day I totally disgraced myself. Our geography teacher, of whom we were genuinely fond, had been killed and Inge and I had to flank the coffin and carry the wreath. Was it because we were so emotionally in-volved? Was it because we so nervous? I do not remember what triggered it, but we both got the giggles, uncontrollable, unstoppable. We stood on that stage, heads bowed, giggling so much that we were shaking. We were really sad, but we could not help ourselves. People thought we were shaking with sobs so somebody kindly relieved us of the wreath and we ran off into the toilets, hooting with hysterical laughter.

In the autumn of 1944 my father decided to have a bunker built, officially for the storage of documents, but really, I think, to keep his family safe from a nuclear attack. A slanted tunnel was excavated into the hill behind our and the neighbour's grounds, leading some 20 metres or so into rock. At the end of it was a bend of 90 degrees, then came a chamber, protected at both ends by steel doors. This chamber had shelving on which stood a few metal canisters, presumably containing the documents. Another short tunnel, another 90-de-gree bend, another solid steel door again and you arrived at our shelter. It had an air filtration plant and lights, both run by a small generator. Equipped with canned food and water, furnished with camp stretchers, table and chairs, our neighbours and we could have survived in there for a week or two at least. It was finished only a couple of months before we had to flee from Bad Harzburg and so we did not use it much. It was creepy and claustrophobic in there, with the hill looming above and no noise apart from the dripping of water seeping through the rock.

The shelter was supposed to be a secret place, but everybody knew about it, of course, as machinery and workmen had made a daily commotion for weeks. The workmen were 15 Russian prisoners, who arrived with their elderly guard every morning at eight and departed every evening at five. We had not really taken much notice of them, until the day when my little sister Sigrid and her friend Bienchen from next door sat on the stone wall, eating fruit they had picked from the old apple tree, and watching the Russians at work. When the little girls came across a wormy apple, they threw it down and were surprised to see a prisoner pick it up and eat it, worm and all! They threw all the apples they had gathered and the Russians devoured them in a flash. Frightened, Sigrid and Bienchen ran inside and told Helene and my mother.

They went to talk to the guard. His charges were hungry, the guard said. Their rations were not adequate. He and his wife did their best to feed them, but there was only enough for two meals a day, so they worked for eight hours without eating. From then on Helene cooked a huge cauldron of soup or Eintopf (stew) for them every day, without grumbling, although cooking was not her favourite occupation. Two of the Russians came at midday to carry the food outside to the little summerhouse at the back of the garden, where they sat down to eat. This midday meal was a secret between the guard, his charges and us. He would have got into trouble, he said, if 'they' found out.

CHAPTER 11

Happier Times

We always had traditional Christmas celebrations in our family, with the Advent wreaths carrying one candle on the first Sunday of December, two on the second and so on. The irony of a family dedicated to Nazi ideology observing traditions stemming from the Hebrew religion completely escaped us. After all, the four candles burning on the Advent wreath commemorate the 4000 years of the Diaspora.

The Christmas Eve ritual started at dusk. The door to the Christmas room was locked all afternoon, so that the tree and presents could be set up in secret. The presents my sister and I had for our parents and Helene had to be put outside the door and they disappeared while we washed and changed into festive clothes. We knew the Christmas tree, which had been selected a few days before, was behind the door with the presents we were giving, but there was always that little doubt: Would the Christkindl (Christ child) really flutter down from heaven on golden wings to bless us and the tree and leave our presents there? Mutti (Mum), Helene, Sigrid, Waldi and I lined up in front of the closed door and waited. Vati (Dad) was in the room, playing the Christmas carols. We sang 'Ihr Kinderlein kommet' (Come, all you children) and 'Stille Nacht, heilige Nacht' (Silent Night) and then the little silver bell tinkled as the signal for Mutti to open the door. And just over the threshold lay a tiny golden feather, proof that the Christkindl had really been visiting.

And there, in the middle of the room, stood the Christmas tree in all its glory, candles alight, baubles, tinsel and ornaments gleaming, all the presents heaped around it, wrapped in colourful paper and name tagged. We admired the wonderful sight, then sat down and took turns in bringing the presents to each recipient, admiring each one together as it was unwrapped. Later in the evening we had wine, tiny glasses for Sigrid and me, and as much marzipan,

Lebkuchen (gingerbread) and other special cookies as we liked. The formal Christmas dinner on the 25th usually featured a roasted goose, Blaukraut (sweet and sour red cabbage) and Knödl (dumplings).

One Christmas stands out in my memory as drastically different. We were lined up before the door, listening to Vati playing and singing, joining his rich baritone with our feminine warbling, when suddenly there was a crash and clatter in the Christmas room. Had the Christkindl crash-landed? The playing and singing had stopped abruptly and there were now the sounds of scraping and rustling and muffled, but audible swearwords, most unChristmas-like, from behind the door. Mutti opened it, cautiously, and there was Vati on his hands and knees, retrieving the smouldering candles from wherever they had landed when the Christmas tree had crashed on top of the table and the wine glasses and the Christmas goodies, which were now scattered. How had this mess come to pass? Well, he had bought a Persian rug as a present for Mutti and had arranged it artistically under the tree. While playing the carols, he had noticed a wrinkle in the rug and from the piano stool stretched out a foot to smooth it away. Chaos ensued.

It took us a while to restore order and regain the Christmas spirit, but it seemed very funny later on, when it had been established that the Persian rug had suffered only a tiny black burn mark, hardly noticeable in its colourful pattern.

When we celebrate Christmas now, nearly half a century later, in our little farmhouse in New Zealand, our family still cherishes the traditional Christmas I remember from my childhood. We exchange presents on Christmas Eve and we have real candles on our tree. We light one candle each for the members of our family who are no longer with us.

Until the early stages of the Second World War it was customary for infantry and artillery officers to be mounted and my father was a good horseman. I inherited his love of horses and passed it on to my daughters. One of my earliest childhood memories is sitting high up in the saddle, in front of my father, being held by him as we flew over a grassy meadow. I can still feel the wind stinging my face and hear the thudding of the hooves, but realise now that the 'flying' was probably no more than a gentle canter. Many of my childhood photos show the horses and foals I was allowed to ride and love. In the earliest photo I am about three years old, astride Rudi, my father's horse, in the Tiergarten in Berlin. There are photos of me on a heavy grey artillery horse, photos of the foals and finally the one where I am sitting on the first steed I owned, my rocking horse, also called Rudi.

I cannot recollect any riding from 1939 to 1944. Then I was lucky enough to be able to groom and have formal riding instructions at the Hannoverian Stud establishment at Bad Harzburg, which had been relocated to be out of danger from bombing raids. It was there that I learned to ride 'properly'. Although riding lessons for girls were frowned upon as being frivolous in times of war, I was fortunate enough to gain entry into the stud's riding school, which trained horses and their riders for ceremonial occasions. My father's friendship with the stud master probably had something to do with my being accepted for the school. Once a week I groomed, mucked out stables, cleaned tack and rode.

Bashyn, the horse assigned to me on grooming days, was a Polish stallion, a beautiful and aristocratic grey, which meant that he was pure white – or supposed to be. Bashyn was kept in a loose box that had thick sawdust on the floor. Bashyn liked to roll. He did not like to be groomed and he was especially sensitive when he was brushed near his private parts. He bit my rear end as I bent down to brush his belly and it was an act of courage to brush his hindquarters and comb his long tail, as he was free with his heels as well.

The old sergeant in charge of stables set very high standards. During an inspection he would run his white gloved hand along the inside hind leg of Bashyn, who of course stood to attention for him. The slightest smudge or speck of dust on the glove meant I had to do another 20 minutes of grooming, with Bashyn reverting to his irritable temper as soon as the sergeant departed. Many bruises later I learned the secret of keeping Bashyn happy: he was addicted to willow branches. Supplied with a stoutish willow branch, he would mouth and chew it contentedly with a faraway look in his eyes and I could even pick up his feet in safety while he snorted and dribbled.

We always rode in the indoor arena. Hands down, hands steady, hands light, toes in, sitting deep in the saddle, knees and calves in contact, back straight, head up, looking beyond the horse's ears, remembering all this, listening to the sergeant's commands and keeping to the prescribed distance between your horse and the others. The sergeant stood in the middle, his lunging whip at the ready. One mistake by rider or horse and he flicked it to touch the ground just beside the culprit. Another mistake and he flicked it to touch the rider or the horse, usually the rider. 'Most faults are riders' faults,' he said. The horses knew his teaching methods and we, the riders, knew too. We took care not to make the same mistake twice. Hohe Schule (dressage) riding involved intricate patterns of direction and paces. Mirrors at the long ends of the arena reflected our movements. If we got it right, the horses were dancing and hardly seemed to touch the ground. It was bliss!

CHAPTER 12

Growing Up

Looking back now, more than 50 years later, I am astonished at the number of incidents from my schooldays I remember. Many of them reflect the turbulent events impacting on me and my family, but others are of very ordinary feelings and happenings in my life during the teenage years.

The new boy had unsettled me. With thick blond hair like a helmet, dark brown eyes, of athletic build and very self-assured, he had sauntered into the classroom. Until then, I, too, had been self-assured, certain of my popularity with classmates, certain of the effect I had on boys, certain of the loyalty of close friends. I was reasonably pleased with myself. The way my long brown hair curled above my shoulders, the way my eyebrows arched, the way I could make my dark blue eyes convey my moods and wishes – all quite satisfactory. True, in spite of years of wearing braces, my teeth were still not as straight as they should be and I was perhaps a little too well rounded on the hips, but all in all not bad.

One Sunday afternoon, a group of my friends was lounging on the grass by the side of the swimming pool, chatting and laughing, the new boy the centre of attention. But I was just one of the crowd as far as he was concerned, that was plain to see. In spite of wearing my new togs, in spite of my witty remarks, which made the other classmates laugh, in spite of giving him the benefit of my deepest, bluest glances, he ignored me.

'Coming in for a swim?' he said to no one in particular and then, casually, 'I'm going to jump from the high tower.' The high tower – nobody from the class had ever dared to do that! The deep end of the pool sported four diving boards: the 1-metre board to the right and then, on a tower, first the 3-metre board, some concrete steps further up the 5-metre board and finally, way up a steel ladder, jutting out from the platform at the top, the 10-metre board. He sauntered over to the tower and we watched him climbing up, first the steps, then the ladder, quick, sure-footed, without hesitation. For a moment he stood on the platform, lifted his arm in a nonchalant wave, then he walked out onto the board, raised both arms, stretched up and jumped. He flew through the air, straight as an arrow, arms outstretched above his head, feet together – a perfect dive. There was hardly a splash as he entered the water. A trail of bubbles marked his underwater swim to the edge of the pool, right to the spot I had run to. And there he was, vaulting up onto the edge, flicking his hair back into its helmet shape.

A few drops of cold water landed on me, making me gasp. I blushed when he looked at me, was annoyed at myself for blushing and felt myself blush even more. 'I'm going for another dive. Anybody coming with me?'

'I'll come,' I heard myself say in a high, squeaky voice.

There was a stunned silence from my classmates and then my best friend Inge said, 'Don't be a fool, you've never been up that high. You can't jump the 10-metre, you'll break your neck!' True, although I was a good swimmer and handled the 3-metre board with ease, the 5-metre board had been a challenge only attempted once, with marginal success.

He was already a few steps away, glancing mockingly back over his shoulder: 'Well?' A challenge? Never could I admit now that this was beyond my capability, that I was afraid. I would lose face in front of my classmates and he would dismiss me completely as a silly, weak female. I was almost angry with him as I followed him, first up the steps, then halfway up the ladder. As the drops from his wet body splashed down on me, I realised I was furious. He had manoeuvred me into this predicament and was probably laughing at me! I wanted to pinch his calves, slap his feet that were just a step or two above my face, but I needed both hands to grasp the sides of the ladder, needed all my willpower to force my trembling limbs up another step and another. Finally I made it to the top. He was already out on the board. Without a backward glance, he stretched up, jumped out and was gone.

Weak of knee and with trembling hands I stood on the platform, holding onto the railing. A few deep breaths would, I hoped, fix the feeling of nausea, of vertigo, of sheer terror. Far, far below I could see him already getting out of the pool, the cluster of my classmates, Inge, my best friend, mouthing something and waving. I tried to wave back, casually, but found I had to grip the rail too quickly again for the gesture to be effective. I looked down again, which was a mistake. The abyss drew me, down into the tiny blue patch of water, down to drown, down to die. I visualised it all: I would stumble and slip on the springboard, fall sideways to hit my head on the 5- and 3-metre boards, and then hurtle into the water. Finished. Could I climb back down? And be laughed at? Pitied? No! Anyway, I probably couldn't climb down the ladder backwards; with my sweaty hands and feet I was bound to slip and fall and be mangled and killed that way. No, there was only one way down: I had to jump.

I stood on that platform for an eternity, until the shallow breathing had stopped and I felt myself going numb. Not hearing or seeing anything beyond the next step my feet were taking, I shuffled to the edge of the board, shakily raised my arms and tumbled forward and down. With a searing pain in my chest, back and head, urgently needing to gulp air instead of water, I thrashed to the surface and reached the side of the pool. My ears full of water, black spots in front of my eyes and very shaky, I was barely aware of Inge's helping hands as she put a towel around my shoulders.

Eventually the shaking stopped. The blurred shapes became individuals again and a I could hear my classmates talking about the dive: 'How stupid! Lucky you didn't kill yourself!', 'You made a big waterspout!' and 'Took you ages to jump. Were you scared? I wouldn't jump from up there.' One voice was absent: the new boy's. He had sauntered off to the dressing sheds.

And suddenly, with a loud bang that reverberated in my head, a bubble burst, water trickled out of my nose and ears, the trembling stopped and sanity and composure suddenly returned. I felt quite calm. The new boy did not matter any more. What mattered was that I felt a new perspective opening up: I was aware now of my strength and weakness. It had taken courage to overcome fear, but it was extremely stupid to be vain enough to do something dangerous, just to impress. It did not matter that I sported two black eyes and suffered from sore ribs for weeks to come: it was the price I had to pay for the insight I had gained.

I fell in love, for real this time. Ernst was in my class, three days a week; on the other days he was away, drafted into the army, manning an anti-aircraft gun. At 16, he was a year older and taller than I and, as his name implied, a serious boy. He was handsome in his grey uniform, with his wavy blond hair, although when I look at his photo now, I see that he had bushy eyebrows and that his dark brown eyes were perhaps a little close together. Poor Ernst, he has been dead for many a year.

He walked me home from school, clipping my schoolbag onto the carrier of his bike and draping his arm across my shoulders. When we could get away from school, home, or war efforts, we went for walks and had serious discussions. My parents did not approve of Ernst and his parents were not too keen on me either, so we could not meet at each other's homes. Sad to say, most of our meetings were more or less clandestine. We swore eternal love all the same and even kissed a few times when saying goodbye at the gate with the 'Z' that led into our grounds. Kissing was not as wonderful as I had expected. Our noses seemed to get in the way, and what with the bike and the schoolbag and worrying if somebody saw us, the expressions of our passion remained somewhat inept and curtailed.

Our affair came to an abrupt end. The love of the century was nipped in the bud by two sets of parents who were endowed with over-active imaginations. Ernst got scarlet fever, was quite ill and ended up in an isolation ward at the hospital. We wrote to each other. He, in his fevered state, waxed lyrical: 'Lass' uns den Kelch der Liebe trinken' (let's drink from the chalice of love), he wrote and I carried his letter around with me, in the breast pocket of my blouse. Unfortunately it was found by Helene, when the blouse went into the wash. Much perturbed, she showed it to my mother, who, even more perturbed, showed it to my father – and then took me for a walk, presumably to talk to me about the facts of life and to find out just how far this great love affair had actually progressed. She was rather vague and I was rather obtuse. I did not really understand what she was getting at and the whole discussion was mutually embarrassing and inconclusive. We were both relieved when our walk was cut short by an air raid.

My father lost no time in getting in touch with Ernst's father. We were forbidden to see each other in future and that was that. Pretty soon Ernst found himself another girlfriend and, not to be outdone, I fell in love with another boy, in a more circumspect way – no love letters.

My mother did not attempt to talk to me about the facts of life again until four years later and even then the dear soul was still beating about the bush. We both chuckled when she realised that I had in the meantime gathered the relevant information about this taboo subject.

From the middle of 1944 on I rose rapidly through the ranks of the BDM to become a Gruppenführerin (group leader). Now I realise that the girls who had been my superiors resigned from their positions smartly when they, or their parents, saw how the war was going to end. Of course nobody talked to me about their motives and I was too naive to see what was going on. I took my duties very seriously. My group of girls, although steadily diminishing in numbers as time went by, marched through town every now and then, carrying banners and singing uplifting songs. We collected pine cones for the elderly and rattled collection boxes for Winterhilfe (winter aid) to help the poor.

Sometimes I came home from BDM meetings in darkness. By six o'clock it was pitch dark during the winter months. I had never been afraid to walk through the park and uphill to our house – until the stalker. There were no lights in the park because of the blackout so I could barely distinguish the paler shade of grey that was the gravel path from the darker shapes of the trees and shrubs flanking it on both sides. Suddenly I became aware that the crunchy sound of my footsteps was echoed by the sound of footsteps behind me. I turned around, could not see anybody and started walking again, faster now. The footsteps were gaining on me. My heart started thumping. I was afraid, but I knew that if I showed fear, I would be very vulnerable. I stopped again, thrust my sweaty hands into my coat pockets, swung around and, in a voice as steady as I could make it, said, 'Hello'. No answer, just the sound of small branches snapping, quite close. Then silence. If only I had something to defend myself with – a stout branch, a biggish stone – but there was nothing. I stood rooted to that spot for an eternity, convinced I could hear my pursuer panting nearby. It took all my willpower to turn my defenceless back on him and walk, pretending to be confident, while the sweat trickled down my back, to the edge of the park, the safety of the street.

There I started running uphill, my heart thumping, his footsteps pounding behind me. At last, the gate! I flew through, clanged it shut behind me and started yelling, 'Helene, Helene!' She was at the door in an instant and we locked and bolted it behind us. It took me a while to calm down enough to tell her about the fright I'd had, but we both decided we would not worry my mother with the incident. She had enough to cope with: my father was away at the time. We would tell Pavlik, my father's driver, when he next came. He was trustworthy, practical and could keep a secret; he would know what to do. He did. He immediately set to and taught me a few survival tricks. 'Never walk close to the side of the footpath. Keep away from fences, shrubbery, buildings and the kerb. Walk with confidence. If you're followed, don't run. Turn and face your pursuer.' I had done most of that, and Pavlik praised me for correct behaviour. But he must have given the matter further thought, because a few days later he presented me with a little Beretta handgun and instructed me in its use. 'Keep it in your pocket. Keep the safety catch on. Shoot only when you're in extreme danger. Use it only at close range. Don't show your gun, but keep your hand on it. You can fire through your pocket, if necessary. If you're attacked, shoot first. Aim for the middle of your attacker. Bulk is easier to hit. If you have time, crouch, or at least present yourself sideways. You're a smaller target that way. Take the gun with you, when you're out after dark on you own,' he said, 'but swear not to tell anyone that you have the Beretta. This is strictly between you and me.' I kept my word and did not tell; I carried the gun in my pocket, as instructed, and I felt invincible.

When I think of Pavlik now, he appears to me as an incarnation of a faithful medieval vassal, the trustworthy soldier who was always ready to serve, ready to fight, ready to die. Of medium height, he was muscular and swarthy with high Slavic cheekbones, very deep-set eyes and always a shadow of dark stubble around his jowls. His cap was usually worn at a rakish angle and his boots were not as shiny as they should have been. A superficial glance might have categorised him as just another driver, unless you looked at his eyes: opaque black, fathomless, simultaneously shrewd, quick and dangerous. Pavlik was the best of my father's three drivers; the other two were elderly but he was in his prime.

CHAPTER 13

The Beginning of the End

On 7 March 1945 the US 1st Army crossed the Rhine at Remagen. During the following weeks the battles fought on German soil came closer and closer as the Americans advanced eastwards and the Russians pushed towards the west. Suddenly I had to face up to the shocking fact that American troops would reach Bad Harzburg very soon. Lately, the radio news bulletins had often been preceded by cheerful marching music, which meant there was bad news to follow: another strategic withdrawal by our armies, another city devastated by Allied bombing raids. Anybody with any common sense could see that the collapse of our government was imminent. Most people made contingency plans; my family did not. To this day I am not sure why we were so blind to reality. Was it total commitment to the cause? Was it a case of absolute loyalty, of allegiance to the oath that had once been pledged to the Führer? Or did my father hope that the secret weapon, almost ready to be unleashed, would turn the tide of despair at the last minute and transform defeat into victory?

Between reporting to HQ and going back to the front, he had been home for just 24 hours, a flying visit. The news had been particularly bad that day: the Russians were advancing towards Berlin and the Americans were across the Rhine. We lived within six to seven hours travelling time of either army. When my father was getting into his car to leave, I asked him, 'What do you want us to do if the Russians or the Americans get here?' He stepped out of the car again, took me in his arms, looked at me with a very stern expression and said, 'You're talking treason. Don't even think that way. They won't get here.' He kissed me and was gone.

So were we, my mother, sister and I, a few weeks later, when we heard the rumbling of heavy guns coming ever closer. I think now that my mother, fear-ing we were doomed, determined that we would all die together, with my father.

The last few days in Bad Harzburg, where we had lived for two years, are deeply etched in my memory, as are the events that followed. Wolfgang, our little cousin, had stayed with us during the past year, to be safe from the bombs landing on Offenbach, his home town. His mother, Aunt Rosel, had arrived suddenly, because she felt he was no longer safe with us. When we fled, she stayed in the house, and died there. She shot herself after being frightened out of her mind by the ex-gardener, who had come to loot the place. Her little boy found her. She lingered for two days.

My mother, a registered nurse, had continued to work voluntarily in the hotel turned military hospital just across the road from where we lived, nursing the wounded and maimed soldiers who arrived by the trainload. She was in charge of changing the dressings when the men reached Bad Harzburg. Most of her patients came from the Russian front and they had often been in the Lazarett Zug (field hospital train) for days. Many of them had maggot-infested wounds under their plasters or bandages. Maggots, though, were better than gangrene: they fed on the debris and kept the wound clean.

My mother had great love and empathy for her patients. She did as much as she could to ease their suffering and dying, helped them come to terms with the loss of limbs and abilities.

Often she came home, utterly exhausted and devastated from the horrendous situations she had to deal with, then went back at night to help someone to die, or to live. Almost all the contents of our liquor cabinet and wine cellar went with her, to ease someone through a particularly painful experience. Many of her patients came to our home when they were well enough, in wheelchairs or hobbling on crutches, some able to walk by themselves. A change of scenery was good for their recovery, said my mother. The men adored her.

She thought of the hospital's chief surgeon as our friend; he had often been a guest in our house. Now, desperately afraid, she asked him for sanctuary in the hospital for her two daughters and herself. He declined, saying he could not take the risk. He supplied us with three cyanide capsules instead, and instructions on how to use them. It was simple, really. You put the capsule into the side of your mouth and when you bit on it, you were dead within seconds.

Our cyanide capsules were always instantly available during the next eventful weeks; I wore mine tucked under my clothing in a tiny pouch that hung around my neck. Having the capsules gave us a sense of security: we knew we could opt out, so to speak, play the trump card. Goering did just that, after he was condemned to death at Nuremberg. His small daughter Ebba, I think she was no more than eight at the time, slipped the cyanide capsule into his mouth when she was allowed into his cell to kiss him goodbye.

Mr Deke, a wealthy landowner and former hunting partner of my father, lived in a village north of Bad Harzburg. He suddenly appeared and offered to take our valuables away for safekeeping, saying we had to flee or face certain death within days. My mother, in her innocence, gave him many of her jewels, her fur coats and as many paintings and artefacts as he could take away in his utility truck. We never saw them again.

As a hunter, he was particularly interested in my father's gun cabinet, but he was out of luck there. I had emptied it of all guns and ammunition the day before. The whole lot had been taken to a cache in the hills, where some of my friends were waiting for me to join them. We were going into action as Werewolves. To become a Werewolf one had to swear the oath to be loyal to all other Werewolves, to fight all enemies and to be prepared to lay down one's life for the fatherland. Heady, heroic, exciting stuff! And very secret. I was the only girl in our den of wolves, having qualified by the fact that I could shoot and had access to several rifles, telescopic sights and lots of ammunition. We were going to snipe at and harass whichever enemy occupied Bad Harzburg: Russian or American soldiers would be easy targets for my father's rifles. We would live off the land and be heroes. This certainly seemed a lot more fun than simply taking cyanide. I do not know where the idea came from, whether the other young stalwarts, average age 16, ever became successful werewolves and what happened to my father's expensive hunting rifles. When I met one of the would-be werewolves 30 years later, he was a prominent person and we both tactfully avoided mentioning youthful escapades.

CHAPTER 14

Escape

Fate intervened and I was not destined to become a werewolf. Two days before Bad Harzburg fell to the Americans, we had the chance to escape. A utility van, carrying important documents, was to leave for Berlin in 15 minutes and would pick us up if we were ready, we were told. That gave me just enough time to follow my mother's example and put my valuables in a safe place. The hollow bronze bust of Hitler, detached from its base, seemed the perfect receptacle for my jewellery, so Oma's sapphire ring, the filigree gold chain and brooch my father had brought for me from Spain and whatever else my treasure box contained, were inserted into the Führer and buried under the rosebed. No doubt the felonious gardener found the bust straightaway and was thereby inspired to demand more valuables from my unfortunate aunt.

We took our air raid bags containing a few clothes, a bit of food, a little money and our cyanide capsules. I took my little pistol and two clips of ammo. We tearfully kissed our two dogs, Waldi II and Toby, little cousin Wolfgang, Aunt Rosel and Helene, our faithful housekeeper goodbye. Leaving the two Dachshunds was the hardest.

The van turned out to be an old delivery van for a greengrocer. Its interior was completely dark when the back door was rolled down and shut. It had an arrangement of colourful fruit painted on its side, with the words, 'Eat More Bananas'. With the documents packed into dark grey canisters, there was just enough room for three of us to huddle on the floor. To travel from Bad Harzburg to Berlin usually takes no more than four hours; it took us all day. Our driver wisely avoided the Autobahn, which was continually bombed and strafed by Allied planes. We trundled along tree-lined country lanes, where we had a better chance of surviving the Tief Flieger (low-flying plane) attacks. After the first narrow escape from being machine-gunned, I became the lookout. Tied by my belt to the rear vision mirror, I squatted on the front mudguard, to spot any low-flying plane approaching from behind. This was quite exciting, although my hands and feet got rather cold and the wind stung my eyes as I squinted into the sky. The planes came upon us very quickly, the drone of their engines hard to hear above the motor noise of our van – just a glint in the sky and there they were! Three times we abandoned the van in a hurry, diving into the ditch beside the road, and we were lucky each time.

We made it into Berlin just before dusk and just before the nightly air raid. The van's driver dropped us off at one of the city's bunkers. I remember long concrete corridors, lit by orange lights, with bunks on each side, four tiers high. Exhausted, we fell into ours, clothes, bags and all. The next morning we made our way to the Hauptquartier (headquarters) in the bunker where Hitler was to die a few days later and where Goebbels had five of his children brought to him, one by one, poisoning them with cyanide before he took the fatal capsule himself.

We had to walk quite a long way because public transport had ceased to operate in Berlin. The Russian Army entered the city a few days later and we could hear big guns rumbling in the distance. Dirty, tired and hungry, we picked our way around bomb craters, over piles of rubble, through muddy streets where water mains had burst. On both sides of the winding paths were skeletons of shattered buildings, mountains of bricks and concrete, twisted metal and splintered wood – a cold, dark miasma of despair, fear and death. An all-pervading stench, constricting your breathing, was witness to the fact that hundreds of the citizens of Berlin lay dead in and under the ruins of their homes.

Forty years later, when visiting the huge cemetery and memorial to the 22,000 Soviet soldiers who fell in the battle for Berlin, I choked back tears. So many young men, far from their loved ones, lay buried in batches under neat concrete slabs. The memorial bore words like honour, glory, freedom, sacrifice, etched in gold lettering. Was this a consolation for their families back home? I hope so. At least there was a memorial to them. There was none for the German civilians who also died in the battle of Berlin, let alone the soldiers. I wonder how many thousands of them perished. They, too, fought and died with those words burnt into their minds.

We made it to headquarters with our last ounce of determination and were rewarded with good news. Yes, our father was still alive, with the Division

Prinz Eugen making his way into Austria, on strategic retreat. Yes, we could still make our way south to meet up with him; there was a bus leaving from barracks on the outskirts of Berlin today, carrying some personnel and, once again, documents to Munich. Bundled into a staff car, we careered away to the army base. There the cook gave us Eintopf (stew) in the mess kitchen, our first hot meal since leaving home. He also, compassionately and surreptitiously, put a green army issue canvas bag on the floor beside us saying, 'This is to keep you going.' It contained four loaves of Kommissbrot (dark brown heavy bread), a block of cheese and a tin of jam.

The Munich bus, camouflaged under olive green netting, was parked beside some trees at the far end of the parade field. As we were escorted across, the sirens howled suddenly: the midday air raid was upon us. Rapid fire from the anti-aircraft guns of the base, ear-splitting explosions and the whine of bombs raining down. Literally by the scruff of my neck our escort hurled me into one of the trenches that zigzagged across the field. To my right I could hear my little sister crying, also my mother's voice. The bombs, the detonations, the ack-ack-ack of the anti-aircraft guns seemed to go on for an eternity, but we were safe for the moment. As long as you could hear the whine of the bomb, it hit somewhere else. A direct hit on your position came swiftly, a bolt from heaven. No whine.

I found the canvas bag next to me and opened it. There was the bread. I can remember thinking, 'It will all be wasted if we're killed now' and I started chomping on a loaf, very fast. Of the direct hit that killed the people a couple of trenches away to my left I remember nothing. When hauled out of my trench some time later, I could walk on wobbly legs, but I could not hear anything and I could not talk, probably because I had a large chunk of bread stuck in my mouth.

I must have been concussed. I lay on the back seat of the bus, which slowly swayed its way through the night, on country roads again, with its headlights off. There were only five other passengers apart from us – office girls, looking after the documents. Kind fate had offered them escape from the death trap of Berlin, for which they were truly grateful.

The next morning an incident occurred that still demands explanation. The straight tarsealed road, deserted except for our bus, ran for quite a distance along a plantation of pinetrees on the right side. There was a wide gate out of which swarmed several men in airforce fatigues, flagging us to a stop. Cheerful and in high spirits, they brought out bottles of lemonade and bars of chocolate. We told them that we thought Berlin would fall within a matter of days and that we held grave fears for the future. This is what they said: 'Wait and see. In a few days something tremendous will happen that will turn defeat into victory. We have the future in our hands right here. Don't worry.'

They were so sure of themselves, so confident, so capable, that we trundled on our way, reassured. But nothing happened to change the course of history. Germany surrendered and a few months later the atom bomb was dropped on Hiroshima. What was hidden in that pinetree plantation? Did they have the atom bomb there? What prevented them from unleashing the ultimate weapon on London or Moscow? More than half a century has passed. Does the truth about historical events ever emerge, or is the saying 'History is written by the victorious' valid for ever?

As our bus travelled south, the driver noticed a woman standing at the road-side, waving both arms, signalling our bus to stop. Would we give her a lift? She, too, was travelling south, on her way to find her young son, who had been evacuated from Berlin to a village nearby. Of course she joined us and we all agreed to make a short detour east to the village, where her son was bil-leted. This decision proved to be dangerously foolish. On the way our driver became increasingly uneasy: there had been no other traffic on the road for a while and the few houses we passed seemed deserted. A flock of crows on the fallow fields was the only sign of life.

'It's only a little further,' the woman had said, when the first rounds of mor-tar fire split the air and brought us to an abrupt halt. Reacting quickly, our driver reversed the bus, right into the roadside ditch. Stuck! 'Out!' he shouted. 'Take what you can carry! Over there!' Over there was a derelict building in the middle of a ploughed field. We struggled through the slushy snow and mud at breakneck speed. The building, or what was left of it, had been a factory for processing sugar beet – crumbling red brick walls, fragments of roof, some rusting vats and machinery on a concrete floor. In one corner, a metal trapdoor gaped open, exposing an empty square concrete tank below that had probably contained the mashed sugar beet; there was a sickly-sweet odour. Into this tank we all piled and pulled the trapdoor down.

Total darkness and total quietness. We were very frightened. When the driver lit a match every now and then, the flickering light illuminated our ghost-like faces. It was getting dark outside too, and eerily silent. All shooting had stopped. The driver climbed up out of the tank, 'to see what's going on', he whispered. He was back down again within seconds. 'They're coming now,' hoarsely.

Silence, and then we heard them. Running. Some shouting. More running. Very close. What if they found us? A grenade tossed down into the tank? A burst of machine-gun fire? Or would they rape us first before they killed us? I had heard stories of what Russian soldiers did. My mother squeezed my hand, guided it to the cyanide pouch. I knew then what I had to do. As soon as they opened the trapdoor, I would put the capsule into my mouth and bite down on it.

Clanging, grinding noises now, some heavy vehicles rumbling past. Tanks? Theirs or ours? Petrified, we sat stock-still in that tank until dawn, when the driver surfaced for another look. 'Come on up, we'll make a run for it, they've gone!' There were deep ruts criss-crossing the field around the factory and a few shell craters. The burnt-out skeleton of our bus, still smoking, lay lopsided in the roadside ditch. But there was not a soldier in sight. We scrambled across the field in a crouched run, dragging our bags. I got the stitch and it was agony to keep moving. We reached a copse of scrubby trees and rested for a while, then walked on and on until we came to a small village. It seemed deserted then suddenly: 'Halt!' But this soldier pointing his gun at us wore field grey. One of ours! He took us to the command post, located in the village school. They had advanced from the south again during the night and the thrust of the Russian forces was now going in a north-westerly direction.

There was a fire going inside a schoolroom, there was hot soup and the friendly young lieutenant allowed my mother to use his field telephone. As we thawed out and talked and laughed with the soldiers we felt we had a new lease on life. My mother, the determined and resourceful woman she was, managed to get a call through to Dresden, to Burschi, an old friend. She convinced him that we needed transport to Munich immediately and he promised to see what he could do.

Her faith in him was justified. Burschi, bless him, was as good as his word. Within three hours a beautiful bus arrived. It was painted white, with a band of red and black, the German eagle and 'Kraft durch Freude' (strength through joy) adorning its side panels. Inside was a pile of blankets, several cartons of army rations and six canisters of fuel. It had also carried a bicycle, which its driver now mounted, departing with: 'Heil Hitler, she's all yours. I'm off home. Good luck!'

Delighted by this manifestation of good fortune smiling at us again, we hastily climbed into the bus and set off, south to Munich, hoping to meet my father there. The woman who had been searching for her son was no longer with us, but we had a new passenger, the young man I'd wounded.

What had happened was this. With my mother busy trying to phone, we sat near the fire, talking and joking with the soldiers. A particularly gregarious young chap sat just across from me, cleaning his pistol. He was showing off. So was I.

'Beautiful piece,' I said.

'Ja,' he replied, 'shoots sweetly.'

'A Lüger?'

'Ja.' Then, 'But what would you know about guns?'

'Oh, enough,' I replied, with a casual but slightly superior smile. 'Can I have a look?'

'Sure,' he said, 'but ...'

'I know to point it at the ground.' Again casually superior.

And so, with a flourish, he handed the pistol to me. It was much heavier than I expected and it handled smoothly. So smoothly that I hardly felt my index finger touch the trigger. So smoothly that it went off with a resounding bang. The soldier doubled over with an equally resounding yelp: I had shot him in the foot. We found the bullet had gone clean through his boot, through his foot and into the floorboards. He bled a bit, he groaned a bit, but he was not angry with me at all. On the contrary, once the foot was bandaged and he looked impressively wounded, he declared that this was the best thing that could have happened to him. Now his fighting days were over, he had to be sent to hospital and the biggest and best was in Munich, which, incidentally, was his home town. He quickly hopped into our bus and stretched out on the back seat, pale and wan, so that his superior, the young lieutenant, could do little else but let him go.

It was late afternoon before we were on our way south again, avoiding all major roads on which we might encounter troop movements. Wending along country roads, we must have strayed into Czechoslovakia near Pilsen. People at the roadside shook their fists at our bus, conspicuous with its big eagle on the side. After nightfall we made only slow progress. Not daring to turn the headlights on, we bumbled along, stopping frequently to decipher road signs by torchlight.

At dawn we thought we had almost reached our goal. We must have been very close to the outskirts of Munich when our journey came to an abrupt halt: we had run into a roadblock. These soldiers, who ordered us out of the bus, were not friendly at all. They were officious, suspicious and downright antagonistic, and increasingly so, as we, bleary-eyed, tired and confused, answered the questions they barked at us. 'Where had we come from?' When we answered 'Berlin', they declared this impossible: the city was completely surrounded, nobody could get out. 'Why did we want to go to Munich?' That my mother wanted to meet her husband was not an acceptable excuse and they were not impressed by our soldier in need of medical attention.

'Why had the army secretaries deserted their post in Berlin and where were the documents they were allegedly transporting to safekeeping in Munich?' They did not believe our story, that the original bus from Berlin had burnt and the documents destroyed. 'Anyway, where were the papers for this bus? From where had it been stolen? Where had the army rations, blankets and fuel canisters come from?'

By this time my mother's story of Burschi sounded far-fetched and incredible even to me. We were prodded back into the bus by three of the soldiers, submachine guns at the ready. 'They're taking you to Dachau. You can tell them your stories there!' the officer sneered.

Dachau. The concentration camp.

CHAPTER 15

Dachau

The big gates of the high double fences slid shut behind our bus. My mother, Sigrid and I filed into the administration building. I felt cold, stiff and numb, scared. Glancing at the pale face of my little sister I knew she felt the same. Mother stood between us, rigid, chin up, looking straight at the officer lounging back in his chair in front of us. 'I am …' His ice-cold voice cut her off. 'You and your daughters are going into Block D, now.'

A guard escorted us into a small cubicle with a grey concrete floor and walls. There were two sets of three wooden bunks against two of the walls, a square window with black bars high up on the third – too high to look through. The heavy wooden door was locked behind us. We were trapped, like animals in a cage, totally helpless and defenceless. When Sigrid needed to relieve herself, she had to pee into a small sump hole in one corner. There had been no response to our polite knocking and calls. It was cold. We each took a grey blanket from the bunks and wrapped them around us. There was nowhere to sit so we huddled together on the thin mattress of one of the bottom bunks, shivered and waited in silence.

After a very long time the door opened and two guards came in. One carried our three packs, the other a biggish metal bowl, containing thick hot soup. He also had three spoons and three chunks of black bread for us. My mother wanted to speak to them, but the one with the packs put his finger to his lips. 'Quiet,' he indicated. Out they went again and the locks clanged shut. We spooned up the soup and ate the bread, and waited again. I do not know whether we stayed in Dachau for one or two days; I think we were too numb to keep track of time. I remember being taken to the showers by a stout and stern woman. We were issued grey toilet paper and a small grey towel with a red stripe down the middle and there was no soap. On the way to the ablution block we walked across a wide open space where groups of prisoners in light and dark striped garb were pushing and pulling heavy carts. They worked silently. We, too, were silent as we passed them. Nobody seemed to talk at Dachau.

An eerie silence pervaded the place. I felt it in my bones, menacing, grey, numbing and lethargic, cold. More than 30 years later, when my sister came on a visit to New Zealand, we toured the West Coast, staying the night at a motor camp at Greymouth. Our small unit had concrete block walls and two sets of two tiered bunks. At dawn she woke, wild-eyed and whispered, 'We must get away from here, right now, before the camp commandant finds out who we are!' She would not go into the showers but waited out on the road for us to pack up and settle the account at the office. We did not discuss her irrational behaviour. I knew what nightmare she had had.

Deliverance from Dachau came swiftly and dramatically. We heard a commotion outside our cubicle and the door flew open. The officer, who had been so insolently intimidating at our arrival, now stood at attention on the threshold. Major Enz, my father's aide-de-camp, swept past him, kissed my mother's hand in an elaborate show of Viennese charm and announced, 'Gnädige Frau, on orders of General Höfle I am to take you and the young ladies to Sonthofen. Allow me to escort you to the car.' The camp officer clicked his heels and saluted as we went past.

'See to the luggage!' Enz flung back at him over his shoulder. Outside stood the Tatra, my father's black limousine, with both standards mounted on the bonnet, the SS on the left and the division flag on the right. Pavlik, our stalwart driver, saluted smartly, slammed the doors shut after us, slid into the driving seat and accelerated past the guards standing at the double gates. Only when we were well away on the open road, did he slow down, turn to look at us and exclaim with a huge grin, 'Phew, that was a close one!'

Enz deposited us at the officers' training centre at Sonthofen. Glad to have accomplished his mission and, I suspect, to be rid of us, he sped away. Pavlik just had time to wink at me and whisper, 'Have you still got it?' I did. The Beretta handgun was small enough to be concealed inside a rolled-up pair of woollen socks in my pack.

CHAPTER 16

Last Days of the Reich

There were hardly any people at the Sonthofen complex. We stayed there for only a couple of days, so my memories of the place are hazy but I know it was warm, it was comfortable, the sun shone and we felt safe for the first time since we had left home. From Sonthofen we were taken to a chalet at Igls, high up the mountain near the Havelekar, on the mountain range that overlooks Innsbruck, Austria. There we waited for my father.

At the end of April the ground was still covered by a heavy blanket of snow and it had started to snow again during the morning when my sister and I went down to the village baker to buy two big loaves of bread. On the way back, we had an experience that still haunts me. Our path intersected a small road with high banks of snow piled up on both sides. Along this straggled a column of perhaps 20 men in dark and light grey striped prison garb, thin, cold and hungry-looking. With them were two armed guards, one in front, the other at the rear, wearing thick coats and heavy black boots.

We stood still, clutching our brown paper bags with the bread inside. Coming up level with us, one of the prisoners lifted his head, looked at us and reached out a bony hand. Instinctively I stepped forward and held out the paper bag to him. My little sister did the same. In a flurry of arms and legs and hungry mouths the bread was snatched and devoured by the lucky few, who were close and quick enough. In a flash the rear guard was upon them, cursing, kicking and punching with the butt of his rifle. The front guard ran back, grabbed us both and swung us around. Levelling his rifle at us, he shouted, 'Weg mit euch! Schnell!' (Away with you. At the double.) We flailed over the snow bank, afraid to look back, afraid to stop. Regaining the narrow path, we panted up the mountain, sobbing.

My father arrived that afternoon. There were hugs and kisses and more hugs and I saw the tension of the previous weeks flowing out of my mother. She had reached her goal: to be united with him again, no matter what the future held in store. I could see relief and warmth and love in my father's eyes, but also see how tired and tense he was. For the first time I noticed that he was greying at the temples, that his back had lost that straight, flexed look of an accomplished horseman. His shoulders sagged a little. It shocked and hurt me to realise that my invincible hero was vulnerable. We sobbed out the story of the prisoners to him. 'Do something!' we implored. And, tired as he was, he got into the car again, 'to see to it'. When he came back, he said, 'They're staying in the school hall. They're warm. They were issued with blankets and they'll get army rations before nightfall.' The stern set of his jaw indicated that further discussion would not be welcomed.

That evening as we huddled around the field radio set we heard again and again through crackling static: 'Stand by for an important news bulletin.' Then the news came. The Führer was dead. He had shot himself in the chancellery bunker in Berlin. The Soviet Army was fighting its way into Berlin, street by street. Admiral Dönitz had been appointed Commander in Chief of our forces and was negotiating a Waffenstillstand (ceasefire) with the Allies.

There was a deathly silence. We did not look at each other. Every person in that little room was wrapped in their individual thoughts. Fear? Sorrow? Relief? Confusion? I just felt stunned, numb, drained of all emotion, as if something big had died within me, leaving me a mere shell. Finally my father cleared his throat. 'We leave at daybreak,' was all he said.

I could not get to sleep that night. My throat was tight and my eyes smarted and it was hard to breathe, but I knew I must not cry, must try to be strong. I could feel my little sister huddled in her blanket beside me, shivering convulsively. I reached across and we clasped each other's hands.

The next day, on our way from Innsbruck back into Bavaria, across the pass and along the Achensee, our small convoy made only painfully slow progress. We became entangled with column after column of military vehicles, remnants of the divisions on their way north from Italy and fragments of the divisions retreating west from Vienna. There were frequent attacks from light aircraft, the ack-ack-ack of their guns and our anti-aircraft fire splitting the air. Numerous burning trucks and cars were pushed to the sides and over the banks of the narrow road. Many soldiers and civilians were also threading their way through this confusion, going in both directions.

Somehow in the mêlée, I cannot recollect how, my sister and I ended up travelling in Enz's car, separated from our convoy. Enz got more and more agitated as the day drew to its close. At dusk he made his driver turn into a small side track. A few hundred metres into the forest we came upon a clearing, a snowy Alpenwiese (alpine meadow) in the middle of which stood a Heustadl (hay barn). The ladder to its loft was attached to brackets on a side wall. To our surprise and consternation, Enz took the ladder off, climbed up to the loft and, after briefly rummaging around inside, encouraged us to climb up after him. The driver struggled up behind us with our packs. 'You'll be safe here until the morning,' Enz said. 'On no account move. Don't let anybody see you!'

Sigrid and I were too confused to argue with him and they were gone in an instant, putting the ladder up on its brackets again. There was a full moon and we could see enough to make a nest in the loose hay. It was cold and quiet. We snuggled into our blankets, clothes and all, and pulled more hay over the top. Although we were hungry and scared, we got the giggles when we thought of the fairy tale of Hänsel and Gretel who had been abandoned in a forest too. They'd got out of their predicament, hadn't they! We drifted off to sleep.

Sometime during the night I woke suddenly, hearing a scratching, thumping noise. Somebody was leaning the ladder against the opening of the loft. I sat up, grasped my Beretta, took the safety catch off and held it steady with both hands, arms outstretched in front of me, right index finger on the trigger – just as Pavlik had taught me. I heard a soft thud, thud as somebody stealthily climbed up the ladder, and heard the loud thud, thud of my heart thumping. Now there was a silhouette in the opening – head and upper body. I fired three times, rapidly. There was a yell and the crash of the ladder falling, then silence.

I had two bullets left in the chamber. Would he come again? Had I killed him? Were there others? We both sat bolt upright in our nest of hay for ages, hardly daring to breathe. Finally, when dawn had broken, I summoned up enough courage to crawl to the opening to peer outside. Nothing there. Only the ladder lying in the snow, a lot of footprints and a few spots of blood.

We did not move until we heard a car approach. It was the the Tatra, my father's big black limousine, driven by Kurt and accompanied by the driver who, together with Enz, had deposited us in the hay barn the night before. 'Quick,' shouted Kurt as he put the ladder up and we scrambled down and jumped into the car. We kept quiet about the scary incident of the night. They took us back to where our convoy had stalled on the road along the Achensee. Relief on both sides when we rejoined our parents!

There was no time for explanations. We had to keep going to reach the border into Bavaria, a few kilometres away. Trying to manoeuvre us past the other convoys, which were blocking the road, proved to be a task almost beyond my father's ability. It came as a shock to us that his commands no longer brought instant results. He had to resort to shouting himself hoarse and waving his arms. Every occupant of every vehicle on that road had his own agenda: to get where he wanted to go in a hurry, not to be killed in the last few days of the war, to survive. It became obvious that my father could not meet up with the Division Prinz Eugen on their way north from Hungary to Germany, but we made it across the border to the first village on the Bavarian side, Kreuth.

Enz was no longer with us. He had deserted, after leaving my sister and me in that barn. Debonair Enz, who used to convey his salutations to my mother with Viennese best manners: 'Küss die Hand und ein charmantes Heil Hitler für die Gnädige Frau' (A kiss on the hand and a charming Heil Hitler to the gracious lady). Enz, who had always been so immaculately attired in tailormade field grey, braided hat at a jaunty angle, knee-high riding boots with spurs he clicked with panache, had left all his finery in a heap on the back seat of his car. Enz had found the driver's dirty overalls from the boot a suitable substitute in which to high-tail it into the Austrian mountains.

I hope he made it home to Vienna and prospered. He was never cut out to be the heroic warrior fate had type-cast him to be; he was rather more like a stage hero of a Strauss operetta and must have found some of the orders he had to obey irksome. My father had sometimes teased him about his boots and spurs: 'Enz, please ride back into the dining room and retrieve the documents I left on the table' – and Enz would click his spurred heels as he went through the door.

CHAPTER 17

Kreuth

K reuth, a picturesque mountain village near the Austrian border of Bavaria, is surrounded by alpine meadows, wooded hills and craggy mountains, the closest of which is the Leonhardstein. Kreuth has been protected by its patron saint, St Leonhard, for the past 900 years or so. In 1945 it was inhabited by about 800 souls, most of them farmers. The wealthiest owned herds of up to 20 dairy cows and most had small parcels of forest which they logged in winter. Also in the village lived a sprinkling of well-to-do folk who had retired to a rural lifestyle, as well as a contingent of refugees from bombed cities or countries already overrun by the Allies.

Kreuth had a hotel, which sported a swimming pool, several guesthouses, a few modest shops on both sides of the Weissach River, a post office, a council office, the Zollhäuser, where the border guards lived, a schoolhouse and of course the Leonhardikirche, the Catholic church up on the hill, which was surrounded a the cemetery and overlooked the village centre.

Kreuth also contained the sanatorium, a complex of buildings where, before the war, the well-to-do had taken the cure, enjoying ill-health in style. The sanatorium had been requisitioned by the military and in 1945 catered for some 200 invalid soldiers, who were suffering from chest wounds. The mountain air was supposed to be good for their lungs, aiding recovery.

It was 2 May 1945. General Patton's Americans were 10 kilometres north of Kreuth, pushing south towards the Austrian border. At the border a remnant of an SS Totenkopfverband (Death's-Head Battalion) had gathered, determined to fight to the bitter end. Kreuth lay roughly in the middle of the two forces.

My father, having deposited his family with the Bürgermeister of Kreuth, was of course concerned for our safety and tried to avoid the village becoming a battlefield. He drove away to negotiate with the American forces, hoping to have the village declared a Red Cross zone on account of the sanatorium. The Americans, probably a trifle battle-weary too and not keen to suffer casualties in the last days before total surrender, agreed, provided the Death's-Heads retreated to Wildbad Kreuth, the spa just north of the Austrian border, and stayed there until the surrender terms were signed. The village of Kreuth had to promise not to offer any resistance and every house had to signal surrender by displaying a white flag. Away south my father sped, trying to talk sense into the Death's-Heads and to persuade them to honour this agreement.

My mother, sister and I waited, and met the residents of the Bürgermeister's villa. There was the Bürgermeister's third wife, an eccentric, but quite likable artist, and her daughter Pücki, the same age as me, who became a close friend. There was the bombed out Schmidt family, husband, wife and infant son, who had set up home in the attic. There was Roeslie, the cook and, most important, the Bürgermeister himself, 81 years old, a professor of medicine and owner of the sanatorium. The villa was a two-storeyed building, with an elegant turret-cum-balcony structure jutting out from the attic. It stood on an embankment above the village, easily visible from the main street below.

We heard the first American tank rumbling along the main street and a loud-hailer announcing the surrender terms. A helmeted soldier, head and shoulders above the open hatch of the tank, surveyed the white flags of surrender: sheets, towels, tablecloths billowing from the windows of all village houses.

All, that is, except the house on the embankment. Now it showed a white flag, now it didn't. The tank slowed and watched. Hidden from its field of vision, the battle of Kreuth was raging between the professor and his third wife. She had sped upstairs, ready to wave a white tablecloth from the balcony window, only to have it wrested from her arms by the enraged professor, who shouted that neither he nor any member of his household would surrender to these cowboys! Third wife was the more agile and wily of the combatants; he, inspired by patriotic rage, was the stronger. The tablecloth fluttered in and out of the window as they fought. We watched in awe and with increasing anxiety. The tank watched too. It had stopped and closed its hatch. It swivelled its gun around. Two ear-splitting rounds of fire and the roof of the little turret was in shreds. At that the other members of the professor's household swung into action. Mr Schmidt and his wife raced upstairs, overpowered the old die-hard and bundled him and his wife out of harm's way. Roeslie snatched two sheets from the master bedroom upstairs and fluttered them out of both windows, indicating to the tank that we had really and truly surrendered this time. Twice.

My mother was left coping with the wriggling and bawling infant Schmidt and we three girls got the giggles. It was relatively peaceful for a while afterwards. Mr Schmidt had locked the professor into the upstairs bathroom which was round the back, so only muffled ranting and rattling of the door knob issued from that quarter. Mrs Schmidt had taken junior away to be pacified and fed. Roeslie and Pücki were comforting third wife in her drawing room. My mother, sister and I had retired to the library downstairs and sat there, not quite sure what to do next. Suddenly the french doors were wrenched open by a Death's-Head lieutenant, who leapt towards us, submachine gun levelled. 'Up against the wall!' he shouted. 'Where is he, the traitor? Tell me where he is!'

We stood in front of the wall, silent. I felt myself getting cold and rigid. I did not dare to move, did not dare to look at my mother and sister beside me. But I knew I would not tell him where my father was. And neither would they.

He prodded the gun at my sister. 'Tell me!'

And she, 11 years old, a skinny little kid with knobbly knees, defied him, flung at him the worst word she knew: 'Scheisskerl!' (shithead) she hissed.

Suddenly there was Pavlik, our driver, at the open doors. Pavlik, our friend! He, too, had a submachine gun levelled at us. He shouted, 'I know where he is! Follow me, Kamerad!' And the Death's-Head swung away from us and crashed after Pavlik, through the french doors, across the lawn and out of sight. We heard a burst of machine-gun fire in the distance. My father turned up a long time later, with Pavlik.

In the cemetery behind St Leonhard's church there was a grave without a name. 'Unknown Soldier, May 1945' read the inscription on the plain wooden cross. My mother often put flowers there and always a green wreath and a candle on All Saints Day. She thought it might be the grave of the Death's-Head lieutenant, who had probably been shot by Pavlik. But more than 20 years later, a successful lawyer from the Rhineland appeared at her door. It was the former Death's-Head. He told her that he had been haunted by his past and asked for her forgiveness.

'Would you have shot us?' she asked him.

'Yes,' he said. That was what haunted him – that he was prepared to shoot a woman and her two children in a moment of panic. My mother, relieved to find him very much alive and not, as she had thought, shot dead by Pavlik and mouldering in his grave behind the church, did forgive him.

CHAPTER 18

Occupation

Germany surrendered unconditionally to the Allies on 5 May 1945. An American officer in his jeep had come to take my father away. 'I have done nothing to be ashamed of, I am not a criminal,' are the words most vivid in my memory of the farewell we bade each other. I did not fully comprehend then what he meant.

A strange visitor, snake-like in appearance and manner, appeared a few days later. We disliked and mistrusted him almost on sight. He said he had a submarine waiting that would take us to Argentina; my father would follow. Someone would call for us that night. We said no to his proposal: we would stay right where we were, awaiting my father's return. Naively, we thought that this would be a matter of weeks, or months at worst. There was a vacuum now; we were in limbo. We did not know how life would go on, what lay in store for us.

Both drivers, Pavlik and Kurt, took their leave. 'I'll be back,' said Pavlik as he hugged me goodbye. 'I'm going to get my sister out.' 'Out' was across the borders of Slovakia. He drove off in the Mercedes, the faster of the two cars. On his way there, Pavlik and the Mercedes were conscripted by an American colonel. Pavlik, the pragmatist, served his new boss well for the next few years, biding his time, and eventually did manage to smuggle his sister and her husband out. More than four years later they all turned up at Kreuth, where they settled and ran a successful Lebensmittel Geschäft (grocery shop) on the main street. Pavlik lies buried a few metres away from my mother's grave, in the new cemetery of Kreuth, down near the Weissach River.

Pavlik's departure left Kurt and the Tatra. We had no further use for a chauffeur-driven limousine. 'Would it be all right to take it home?' Kurt asked. It would be an ideal car to start a taxi business with. 'Take it,' said my mother. 'Drive carefully and good luck.' She always advised everybody to drive carefully, but poor Kurt was not careful enough. On his way home to Bad Harzburg he was stopped at the checkpoint between the American and British zones. He had a photo of my father in full uniform stashed away behind the sun visor. 'To my faithful Kurt with every good wish' was written on the back, over my father's signature. Naively, Kurt had hoped to use the photo as evidence of his ownership of the car. Alas, the Tatra was confiscated as war booty by a British officer and Kurt was incarcerated in a de-Nazification camp. (There were many of these camps dotted about the American, British and French zones of Germany. One of the common sayings of the time was that every German male between 20 and 80 had either been in a concentration camp, was inside a concentration camp at present, or was just about to be taken into one.)

Old Professor März had also been taken away by helmeted 'Amies' (Americans) and Mr Schmidt had prudently disappeared, 'just in case', so we were a household of women at the villa. The Americans must have considered us very dangerous people nevertheless. They put up a large tent on the front lawn from which a contingent of six soldiers kept a wary eye on us. We kept a wary eye on them too, locking the french doors and keeping all windows on that side of the house firmly shut. An uneasy stalemate lasted for a week or so. We found out later that they were all young lads from Texas and that they had firm orders forbidding them to talk to, let alone associate with, any German over the age of 10 years, because all these people were contaminated with Nazi ideas. Armistice or not, all Germans were still the enemy and on no account to be trusted.

But in this household there was Roeslie, the cook, rosy Roeslie bustling about, passing the tent on her way to and from the vegetable garden, Roeslie, buxom, friendly, happy and nubile. True, she was older than 10, but surely she was not too badly contaminated … The sergeant was obviously charmed by her, and Roeslie was interested in him too. A cautious friendship developed and this led to a more relaxed attitude between them and us.

A terrific thunderstorm led to the next phase in German/American relations. Forked lightning, deafening thunderclaps reverberating around the mountains, sheets of rain and finally snow, proved to be too much for the Texans to endure in their tent. When rivulets of ice-cold water soaked the floor of their tent, they'd had enough. A knock at the kitchen door and in they trooped, put their guns in the umbrella stand in the hall and settled down for a cosy get-together with the enemy. We got on just fine after that. They taught us to sing 'Deep in the Heart of Texas' with the appropriate hand-clapping actions and we taught them the Bavarian Kuckuck song, with finger snapping. We taught them canasta, they taught us poker. We now thought of them as 'our Texans' and they probably thought of us as 'our Germans'. They often supplied us with much appreciated army rations.

Visits from other members of the US forces were not quite so sanguine. Jeep loads of officers arrived at frequent intervals to search the villa, usually also to 'souvenir' valuable items that took their fancy. Our Texan sergeant had to accompany them on their searches, during which he always was ill at ease. On one of the earliest searches he happened to open the drawer of my bedside table where, rolled up in a pair of socks, he found my Beretta pistol. 'Yours?' I nodded. 'I won't find anything here when I come back to search tomorrow,' was all he said. The death penalty was in force at that time for concealing firearms. As soon as they were gone, I put my precious little gun into a biscuit tin and hurried up into the wood behind the villa. There I buried it beside a big beech tree. I never found it when I looked for it a long time later, but then again, I was no longer sure which beech tree had been its hiding place.

During the first few searches, Mrs Schmidt, who lived in the attic, also harboured a guilty secret. She confessed to the rest of the household that she had a soldier hidden behind a sliding panel which led from her room into roof space. The unfortunate man had deserted during the last days of fighting and had been on his way home, when he was trapped at Kreuth. He had kept very quiet up in the attic. Every time there was a search, Mrs Schmidt pushed her baby's cot across the panel and somehow enticed the infant to bawl with gusto. The searchers never lingered in her room. Eventually the soldier found it safe enough to disappear during one dark night, much to Mrs Schmidt's relief.

After the silver tea set had been souvenired by an American officer, we buried the rest of the silverware under the potting shed in the vegetable garden. When the officer in charge of the next search party opened the cutlery drawer, there was only tin cutlery nestling in the velvet compartments. 'We're all allergic to silver in this house – touching silver brings us out in spots. Big red spots all over. You'll not find any precious metal here at all,' stated my mother firmly. He had to be content with taking the last china ornament, a figurine of a Dresden shepherdess, instead.

The summer of 1945 was, in spite of all that had happened in the preceding month and in spite of present hardships, quite a happy time for my sister and me. I think it was because, having survived the end of the war, we felt very much alive and relieved that the stressful times of our flight and all the horrendous experiences of the last months were behind us. It was all over. This should have been a time of reflection, a time to re-evaluate previously held convictions and opinions, but I did not want to think and reflect. There were so many new impressions and so many unfamiliar scenarios to absorb. We had been catapulted into a totally different lifestyle and there was a newfound freedom to do more or less as we chose. Schools had not yet reopened and our mother was occupied with her own worries and problems.

It must have been tremendously hard for her to realise that the ideology she and my father had believed in and had been faithful to had not only proved to be wrong, but had also led to incredible suffering for millions of people. This and the internment of my father, somewhere unknown, as well as coming to terms with our changes in status, location and wealth, were more than enough for her to cope with, quite apart from the day-to-day problems of finding food and clothes.

The practical difficulties certainly loomed large. Food, or the lack of it, was the most urgent. In the surrounding alpine meadows we picked large amounts of stinging nettle and Sauerampfer (sorrel) to eat as spinach, dug out some pretty mouldy potatoes from the compost heap of the sanatorium and were often helped by kind donations of eggs and milk from the local people, who remembered that the unscathed condition of the village was due to my father's efforts.

As newcomers, we needed ration cards, which entitled you to buy the minimum weekly amount of foodstuffs required to keep you alive. I recall this to be 50 grams of fat, 200 grams of meat per week and just enough bread to allow for four thin slices per day. The bread contained a fair amount of potato and maize flour and went mouldy in a day or two.

When my mother applied for the issue of ration cards at the office of the occupation authorities she was told that she was not eligible as she and her daughters were Nazis. When she tried again a few weeks later she was told to wait until her request was reconsidered. And so she waited, sitting on the steps outside the office all day. She came back and sat there the next day. On the third day she was joined by a few of the village women, who waited with her in silence. On the fourth day, when about 20 women had joined her vigil, the authorities relented and issued her with ration cards.

Getting money to buy the rations was not easy either. The family had been with the Dresdener Bank but Dresden was in the Soviet zone and the bank account was wiped out. We raised a small amount of money by making dolls hand-crafted from bits of wire, scraps of material, strands of wool and dressed in traditional Bavarian costume. The little souvenir shop in the village sold them to American servicemen but they did not sell very well, because, truth to tell, they were of marginal beauty and quality.

Our more successful money-making venture was that of selling firewood from the nearby forest, property of the Duke of Bavaria who had given us permission to forage. The firewood scheme had been the brainchild of my little sister. And that's where our love for and obsession with horses came in.

In the trees at the top end of a sloping alpine meadow, not far from the edge of the village, the remnants of a company of Hungarian cavalry had established camp. About 20 men and some of their families had travelled in horse-drawn covered wagons and carts over the mountain passes and had reached the end of the line at Kreuth. Their horses, ranging from thoroughbred Hungarian stallions to tough and wiry Puszta ponies, drew my sister, our friend Pücki, the daughter of the professor and his third wife, and me like a magnet. The Hungarians were friendly. Sure, we could ride their horses. Indeed we could take a horse or three away with us if we could feed and look after them. Bliss! We rode away with three. Our startled mothers were not quite as enthusiastic when confronted with our acquisitions.

Away behind the grounds of the villa was a row of outhouses, implement sheds and a stable. This was where Blind Sepp lived. Sepp, who had been blind from birth, could only distinguish vague shapes of darkness and light but had compensated for his handicap by a highly developed sense of orientation and touch. About 50 years old, he had always lived there and trundled the sanatorium's rubbish carts and washing trolleys around. Sepp loved horses. It had been his dream to own one. Sigrid and Sepp negotiated with the Hungarians to buy two sturdy Puszta ponies, Gitschi and Lisa; their harness and cart were purchased with Sepp's life savings of 1100 marks. Sigrid and Sepp drove them home triumphantly and announced they were going into business together, carting things. She would drive the team, he would look after them. This was the beginning of our firewood scheme.

There were enough windfall branches in the forest to make gathering them into heaps at the side of the tracks relatively easy work. Sepp snapped or cut the branches into suitable lengths and tied them into bundles. When we had enough to fill the cart, we unhobbled Gitschi and Lisa, who had been grazing at the trackside, hitched them up while Sepp threw the bundles onto the cart and away we went. Sepp had to run behind with one hand on the brake, which had to be cranked tight, quickly, when going downhill, to prevent the cart crashing into the ponies on steep parts of the track. We had a few anxious moments. Once Lisa sat down on her haunches with the harness around her ears, while Gitschi nearly strangled himself in his reins. Much screaming and scrabbling out from under bundles of firewood, harness and wagon wheels on that occasion, but by and large we did pretty well and our firewood business thrived during the summers of 1945 to 1946, bringing in some much needed cash.

From time to time, the Hungarians found it necessary to cull their horses. One horse fed a lot of people, and we were always given a chunk of horsemeat too. 'Lohush,' they'd announce and drop an oozing parcel on our kitchen table. 'It's all right to eat it, if we don't know the horse it came from,' we said to each other, grateful for any extra food supply. The meat was of a dark red hue and the little bit of fat on it had a yellowish tinge, but it tasted almost like beef, if one ate it quickly – which we did.

Late in autumn of 1945 we had the first news of my father: he was in an internment camp near Frankfurt. We travelled to this camp, hoping to see him. We waited in front of the entrance gate to the camp for two days, pleading with the Military Police guards to confirm whether he was really there. To no avail – they would neither confirm nor deny, but were totally impassive and uncommunicative.

We did not feel angry with these guards, we did not feel frustrated, we just felt utterly defeated and exhausted when we left. My mother cried that night and Sigrid and I cried with her. I think it was then that we were afraid of what the future held in store. We feared for my father. Would we ever see him again?

CHAPTER 19

The Moths' Palace

Later in the autumn of 1945 we shifted from the Bürgermeister's villa into the Tillmann Haus, nicknamed by the villagers the Mottenschloss (the moths' palace). A three-storeyed mansion of faded splendour, it now sheltered a conglomeration of people. The former servants' quarters up in the attic, housed a titled relative of the deceased Tillmanns. Now in her thirties, she had 'gone astray', as evidenced by her small blond son. She wore flowing colourful kaftans, wrote epic novels and neglected her son, who was a dear little boy. My mother took him under her wing.

An Anthroposophist, also a titled lady, but of advanced years, lived in spiritual enlightenment in a dark little room on the first floor. She became a dear friend to my mother. Also on the first floor lived two Hungarians. One disappeared into the murky black market scene and the other was taken over by a glamorous blonde of doubtful reputation. The pair had many loud and physical arguments and whenever he lost one of their bouts of fisticuffs, he would come down to us to be consoled. The Schmidt family, who had also stayed at the Bürgermeister's villa, now lived in a large room on the first floor. Mr Schmidt had come back from limbo and found a job, working for the Americans as janitor in the Hotel Post in the middle of the village. On the ground floor near the kitchen lived an elderly couple who were employed as caretakers by the Tillmann estate. They were continually thwarted in their surly attempts to lay down rules and regulations for the multitude of tenants.

For six diverse households to manage cooking what little food there was on one enormous wood-fired range in the huge, stone-flagged kitchen, share one sink, three cold water taps and two toilets in good humour, meant that we all had to tolerate and support one another – but then, too, we were a united front against the caretakers.

The boathouse at Feldafing, on the shores of the Starnberger See, where we were staying in September 1939 when word came that war had been declared.

Plastering Sigrid with sunscreen lotion. We had spent an idyllic month at the boathouse.

With Waldi at Zakopane, winter 1939-40.

My father didn't take us hunting often: Sigrid and I always did our best to frighten off any game.

With Vati frequently away, his occasional visits home were special times for us all.

With Aunt Non-non in Garmisch.

Family at Garmisch in the Bavarian mountains, all dressed appropriately.

Bad Harzburg. The Harzburger Hof is the large building at centre left.

The family at Bad Harzburg. This is
the last photo I have of us all together.

With two of my mother's patients. She
helped to nurse wounded soldiers in
the Harzburger Hof, a hotel that had
been converted into a military hospital.

Kreuth

'Teddy', one of the GIs who camped on the lawn at Kreuth. We thought of them as 'our Texans' and they probably thought of us as 'our Germans'.

Riding Musko, 'my' Hungarian horse and wearing my new, scratchy, bright red shorts made from Third Reich flags.

On the ground floor at one end of the grand entrance hall lived a Hungarian captain with his wife and two little daughters. They kept very much to themselves until they emigrated to France, where they had relatives. We, too, lived at ground level, in a big room with a bay window, complete with window seat, which had once been the drawing room. The room, which could be heated by means of a green tiled Kachelofen that reached almost to the ceiling, had the added advantage of french doors, which opened onto a narrow wooden verandah and then out into the overgrown garden. Thus we had two entrances. The 'proper' one was the door leading into the baronial entrance hall with its black and white marble floor, a curving staircase on the left, a huge antique wardrobe on the right and a moose head trophy above the Hungarians' door, straight ahead. The moose looked at you, sad and moth-eaten, when you entered through the massive double doors of the main entrance.

By decree of the caretakers, the entrance hall had to be kept immaculately clean. Whenever it was our turn on the roster, my sister and I would just slosh two or three buckets of soapy water over the marble and swish the mess down the grand entrance steps – to the displeasure of the caretakers. Our room was furnished with the bare necessities kind people had given us. We had three beds, a low round table, two chairs, a chest of drawers in which we kept a few cooking utensils and our meagre food supply. A wash stand, complete with mirror, a porcelain basin and jug, was hidden in the gap between the two wardrobes, which contained all the clothes we owned. We'd rigged up a curtain there, to give the person performing her ablutions some privacy. Occasionally we also used these washing facilities as a watering trough for our horses, when we were too lazy to walk all the way to the kitchen tap to get a water bucket.

One day, the village priest, Father Engelmann (angel man, that really was his surname!), paid us an unexpected visit, intending to improve our spiritual well-being. Just back from a long ride, we had led a very thirsty horse up onto the verandah, through the french doors, straight to the wash stand. There it stood, back end protruding into the room, front end hidden between the wardrobes, slurping water loudly and contentedly. In answer to our casual, 'Come in', Father Engelmann had opened the door from the hall entrance to be confronted by a horse's behind looming tall. As he reeled back, my sister called out reassuringly, 'It's all right, Father, this is a Hungarian horse. It's Catholic.' Fortunately Father Engelmann had a good sense of humour.

He never flagged in his attempts to save our souls, even going to the extent of physical indoctrination. Once a year in early November Kreuth stages the

Leonhardi Umritt (procession). St Leonhard, the patron saint of the village, is also the patron saint of domestic and farm animals and it has been a tradition for hundreds of years that the villagers parade themselves and their animals three times through the village and past the church to be blessed. The Leonhardi Umritt is still the major event of traditional feast days in the village; the other two are the Blessing of the Fields in spring and the Alm Abtrieb (retreat from the high alpine pastures) in autumn. Only residents of the village are entitled to take part.

For the Leonhardi Umritt the animals are splendidly decorated with garlands, blue and white ribbons and rosettes; the horses have gleaming brasses. The young men ride their farm horses and many of them carry embroidered banners of the saint or the Virgin and of various clubs and institutions. Beautifully adorned cows, calves, sheep and goats, all led by their owners, follow the horses. The decorated wagons are next, one for married ladies, one for Jungfrauen (virgins), one for bachelors, one for old men – all strictly segregated, of course. All participants wear the Bavarian Tracht and the women's long skirts have horizontal stripes in colour combinations identifying the village. The black bodice, tight-fitting with leg of mutton sleeves and a bustle at the back, decorated with silver buttons and chains, is rather low-cut with a 'balcony' in front that holds fresh flowers. A silk apron in a pastel shade or a white linen apron with a lace border is worn over the skirt. A black hat with gold braid and a big tassel at the side completes the women's outfit.

The brass band leads the procession and a straggle of youngsters, riding, carrying or dragging their pets along, brings up the rear. My sister and I used to ride 'our' horses as part of that contingent. Father Engelmann and two altar boys, resplendent in red cassocks and frothy white lace, always stood on the steps leading up to the church. On behalf of St Leonhard, Father bestowed blessings upon all participants of the procession three times as they passed. To facilitate this, the altar boys had buckets of holy water at the ready. Father had a long-handled swishy brush, which he dipped into the water to sprinkle it over people and animals. Whenever Father saw us coming, he took an extra deep dip of holy water and then, taking careful aim, reached up and out, letting us have it with a flourish, so that our eyes smarted and our horses snorted and shied.

CHAPTER 20

The Princess

B ecause of its location, just an hour's drive south of Munich, the capital of the state of Bavaria, and 10 minutes away from the border into Austria, as well as its idyllic traditional atmosphere and picturesque scenery, Kreuth has always been a favourite retreat for the titled, the famous and the wealthy. Wildbad Kreuth, where the Death's-Heads had made their last stand, is still the summer residence of the Wittelsbachs, Bavaria's royal family, who also own large tracts of the surrounding forests. We often rode 'our' horses along the forest paths and that was where we met the Princess.

She wobbled into the village once a week on her old bone-shaker bicycle. Thin, with leathery skin and wispy white hair, she did not bend over the handlebars, but sat upright, back straight, head held high, eyes bright blue and alert. With a faint twinkle of amusement as she acknowledged the greetings of the village folk, she was still a gracious presence, inspiring respect in spite of her threadbare appearance, in spite of her oddity, in spite of her age.

'Grüss Gott, Gnädige,' said the butcher, 'it's all ready for you.' And he charged her a small portion of the ordinary price for her purchase. It was always the same, every week. A few thin slices of pressed meat in a tiny brown paper parcel and a large chunk of ox liver in a bulky newspaper bundle, done up with much string. The little parcel went into the cane basket, which was attached to the handlebars and the liver was securely balanced on the carrier over the back wheel, a task performed by the butcher's assistant, who used more string and much effort, under the supervision of the butcher himself. Away she wobbled, 6 kilometres on gravelled paths, uphill through the forest to her abode. A frugal small wooden chalet, hardly more than a shack, with two rooms inside, a water trough in front of the house and a 'long drop toilet' among the trees at the back, it was one of a series of Jagdhütten (hunting lodges) that belonged to the Wittelsbachs. It was given to her by the present duke, by grace and favour. After all, she was family, even if she was a bit odd. At 82 years of age she was entitled to her bit of eccentricity. The Princess Isenburg of Hessen, cousin to the late Czarina of Russia, related to Queen Victoria of England, as they all were.

'Nice hunter,' she had remarked. 'A bit heavy in the head, though. It must be fun riding bareback. I was never allowed to. Mostly side-saddle in those days.'

We had come across each other on a forest path, she on her bone-shaker, my sister and I on horseback. We rode bareback because we did not own saddles; we were lucky to own the clothes on our backs. 'Come and visit,' she had said, and when we did, she was delighted.

'These ladies are my visitors, Franz,' she called. We did not see Franz and presumed he was one of the many cats that were sharing her residence. There were cats everywhere, black and grey, striped and mottled, thin and fat, old and young. Shy of the visitors, they obviously loved and were loved by the Princess. 'How many cats?' She did not know, but there must be at least 20 she thought. That explained the ox livers.

We partook of china tea, light in colour and taste, from paper-thin cups. No sugar was offered. We visited occasionally from then on, whenever we were riding through that part of the forest. She always seemed glad to see us and the horses. 'Was she lonely?' we wondered. 'Was she safe?' She was old, alone and frail, deep in the forest, and these were turbulent times, with dangerous people roaming about. She did not appear to be the least bit worried, shrugging off our concern as irrelevant.

One late afternoon in the autumn when we called on her, the door was ajar and the cats much in evidence, but there was no reply to our greetings. We sat on the wooden bench under the eaves, our horses tied, as usual, to the nearest fir-trees, and waited, called, and waited again. Suddenly we heard heavy footsteps coming up to the back of the hut, then a thump and silence. 'Hallo?' No answer. Nothing. Somebody was there, somebody had frightened our horses, who were now snorting and stomping and rolling their eyes. Quickly my sister ran to quieten and comfort them while I, riding-switch nervously raised, tip-toed round the corner of the hut. Nothing, nobody, only a heap of freshly cut firewood in front of the wood-pile. A mist was rising; we felt cold and, like our horses, wanted urgently to be away from this place. Riding like the wind, we rushed home, shut the stable door and bolted our own door. We did not tell anybody what had happened, did not even discuss it ourselves.

Many days passed before we wanted to ride in that part of the forest again, and when we did, it was on a bright sunny day. The hut stood serene in its clearing, smoke curled up from the chimney and the Princess sat outside on the bench, reading. She smiled and waved, was glad to see us. Sitting beside her, cups of china tea politely balanced, chatting about this and that, it was obvious that everything was fine and normal. We had been silly to be frightened, neurotic, imagining things. All was well. Until … suddenly there were heavy footsteps around the back of the hut and we froze. 'It's all right, Franz,' murmured the Princess, 'the ladies have come to visit. It's all right.'

And to us, with that amused twinkle in her eye, 'Did he frighten you the other day? No need for you to be afraid of Franz. He knows you'll do me no harm.'

Still somewhat shaken, we asked who this invisible Franz was, but our question was airily dismissed with a vague 'Oh, he has always been with me, keeping me from harm.'

Franz had been her footman in days gone past, we learned later in the village. A faithful servant, he had continued to care for the Princess, long after his wages had ceased to be paid, year in, year out, even when her residence had shrunk to a mere hut in the forest, her equipage to a bone-shaker bicycle. 'Loyal unto Death' was the inscription on the modest cross bearing his name in the village cemetery where he had been laid to rest several years before. The wildflowers wilting in a small jar at the foot of his cross were replaced by a fresh bunch every time the Princess came down to the village, they said. The Princess Isenburg and her Franz. 'Loyal unto Death'. And beyond?

CHAPTER 21

Hard Times

We were in dire straits financially. The meagre amount of Flüchtlings Unterstützung (refugee dole) we received just covered our rent and the bare necessities of food. Not that there was much food to be had anyway; these were hungry years for most people in Germany. We ate Kartoffel Gemüse (potatoes in an onion sauce) and Goldrüben (swedes) day after day, not only because my mother was not an accomplished cook, but because the potato stew and the bread, which quickly went mouldy, was more or less the only food available to us, apart from the occasional gift of horse meat and eggs and milk.

Our clothes soon got rather shabby. Somebody had dumped a pile of Third Reich flags, which were no longer in vogue, at the Bürgermeister's home. We removed the white circle and the black swastika from the middle of the bright red material and sewed skirts and shorts for my sister and me. They were a bit stiff and scratchy to wear and people certainly saw us coming from a long way off, but the material was strong and the garments served us well.

Somehow, we received a box of clothes that had been retrieved from the house at Bad Harzburg. In it were a few items of my mother's clothes, two pairs of shoes, two uniform greatcoats, one of leather, a hunting jacket of my father's and a few dresses and high-heeled shoes that had belonged to Helene, our housekeeper. We did not know where Helene was, or if she had survived the end of the war. The day we fled Bad Harzburg, she left with her love, a wounded Austrian soldier who had been one of my mother's patients; they hoped to reach Steyr, his home town. Seven years later, she found my mother and sister again and there was a joyful reunion. Helene and her Austrian were happily married, had prospered and were the proud parents of a little boy.

Two of Helene's dresses fitted me, although they were a bit short. One winter dress of a brown woollen material had a wide orange stripe across the chest and I hated wearing it, but another one of white satin with red and blue flowers was quite dashing. Helene's feet were smaller than mine, but I squeezed into her shoes anyway when the occasion demanded something more elegant than my only other pair of summer shoes, brown plastic Roman sandals. The higgledy-piggledy crooked toes and deformed feet I hobble around on these days probably originated then.

There had been no further news of my father for month after month and we still did not know whether he had indeed been at the internment camp near Frankfurt, where we had gone in a vain attempt to see him. In the summer of 1946, however, we heard that he was in Internment Camp 78, in Kornwestheim, but our letters to him came back marked 'Verlegt' (transferred). Shortly afterwards we were informed that he had been transferred to stand trial in Nuremberg. My mother worried and suffered greatly during this time, but she never broke down in front of my sister and me.

Because my mother was preoccupied with her own problems, anxieties and thoughts, Sigrid and I lived in almost unfettered freedom. We carted the firewood, we grazed our horses in the Kurpark, the common at the edge of the village, and along the banks of the River Weissach and we rode and rode to our hearts' content. Bareback, of course, and bare-legged too, since we had no riding breeches; we did not mind the rashes on our legs caused by the horses' sweat.

Musko, 'my' mare, was a sturdy and stocky bay who never lost condition or the glossy sheen of her coat, even though she foraged only on roadside grass. I am glad to know that she lived to a ripe old age, well cared for by the farmer to whom her Hungarian owner had later sold her.

Musko saved my life on the day she proved to be a hundred times smarter than I was. We had cantered along a forest path and, when rounding a corner, came upon a barrier, a red and white striped wooden beam, like a railway crossing, right across the track. 'Road closed. Restricted Area. No Entry' read the signs beside it. 'Nonsense,' I thought. 'Come on, Musko, we'll jump it.' And jump it we did. She sailed across with ease but then she was most reluctant to go further. As we minced along, she snorted and tensed, swishing her tail and tossing her head. Suddenly she reared, whirled around and bolted back the way we had come. I nearly fell off and had to hang on to her mane as she jumped the barrier again. We had not raced more than 50 metres down the track when a huge explosion shook the earth. I came off, but managed to hold onto her reins. We were both standing trembling at the side of the path, when an American jeep roared up, the soldiers demanding what the hell I was doing there, could I not read, and so on. There had been an ammunition dump in the forest, and they had just blown it up. Musko, the war horse, had smelt the burning fuse and known that there was danger. She knew that to go further spelt disaster and so she took charge, ignoring the wishes of her foolhardy rider.

The American occupation forces were not really a danger to us: they minded their own business, we minded ours. They even helped us when poor Feketa, the black stallion who had broken his nose when he fell over a bluff, had to be put out of his misery.

'Please help us and shoot our horse, he is too sick to get better.' We had flagged down three soldiers who were driving a jeep down the road near the Bürgermeister's house. They came at once and shot Feketa right where he lay, on the front lawn, near the rose bed. Released from his suffering, he died instantly, and they drove off. We stood there, tearful and stunned. A dead horse is very big and Feketa was not a pretty sight to behold lying in front of the house, near the french doors. The professor's wife and our mother were not pleased with their daughters. The horse had to be taken away and buried, which would require the digging of a big hole, a very big hole. Clearly the front lawn was not the place for this, so we hitched up Gitschi and Lisa, the little wood-carting ponies, attached a lot of ropes and a chain to poor Feketa's corpse and dragged him away to a bank behind the stables where Blind Sepp lived. It took us three girls and Blind Sepp until late into the night to manoeuvre Feketa over the edge and then pile branches and lots of earth on top of him. Later we had to shovel more earth down the bank, every time it rained, because his feet kept sticking up out of the hole as the ground settled. The Hungarians were angry with us too, pointing out that Feketa would have fed a lot of people if they had dealt with him.

The first contingent of American troops left and our Texan friends were replaced by 20 or so black soldiers. Billeted in the middle of the village in the Hotel Post, they had brought their own girlfriends with them, which meant the village girls were not pestered. Their sergeant was a big, glistening and jolly fellow. Every morning he posted himself in the middle of the road in the centre of the village where everybody who passed greeted him with 'Grüss Gott, Sergeant'. He nodded and beamed with his very white teeth, clearly pleased to be acknowledged and respected. All went well until the night when the sergeant and his whole contingent got roaring drunk. They smashed every stick of furniture in the hotel, then made a big bonfire in the courtyard and danced around it, shooting their guns and flares into the air. The next morning, a column of white jeeps arrived and the MPs (Military Police) beat 'our' sergeant and his men with truncheons and took them away. With the exception of the owner of the hotel, everyone was quite sorry to see them go.

Only once was I frightened by black American soldiers. In the winter of 1946, on my way home from a food-foraging expedition to Augsburg, the train I was in was brought to a halt in wide open spaces. Out of the slit in the boarded-up window of the compartment we saw some jeeps full of black soldiers race up to the railway line. The soldiers leapt out, drew revolvers, fired shots at random and shouted a lot. We heard women screaming. The elderly man sitting next to me was quick to sum up the situation. 'They're drunk. They're looking for girls!' He took off his coat, threw it over my head, put his arm across my shoulder and whispered, 'Cough! Keep coughing! Keep your head down!' I did, coughed and choked like mad when two soldiers burst through the door and came to where we sat.. 'My wife,' said the elderly man, 'TB.' They briefly shone a torch at my huddled form and went on into the next carriage.

Eventually the train chugged on. My benefactor did not want to be thanked. 'Nonsense, girl,' he grumbled. 'I've a daughter like you at home. Shouldn't be travelling alone. Stay home next time!' I never told my mother of this incident. She would not have wanted me to travel alone again, but I did not want her to go to Augsburg, to forage for food and be humiliated and face danger.

When the schools reopened, I think it was in September 1945, we had to attend again, reluctantly. It was not so bad for my sister, she just had to walk down the hill to the village school, but my Oberschule (high school) was at the Sängerschlessle in Tegernsee, a good 10 kilometres from Kreuth. I took the railway bus to Tegernsee at quarter past seven in the morning and, weather permitting, walked all the way home to save the bus fare. The little prince often walked with me. He, his father, mother and her lady-in-waiting had fled from their estates in East Prussia one snowy night, running for their lives across ploughed fields. They had only the clothes they stood up in, although the lady-in-waiting had prudently snatched the duchess's jewel case at the last minute. Count Donar of Tegernsee had kindly taken his relations in. They resided in the summerhouse in his park, refined, bewildered and totally unequipped for survival in a harsh and unfamiliar environment.

When most of the jewels had been bartered away to supply the necessities of life, the old duke bravely went to look for employment and found a job as janitor in the American officers' mess. There he cleaned the toilets and washed the floors, stoked the boiler and cleaned the men's boots. For this latter job he got extra tips as the Americans got a kick out of having their boots shined by a real duke. He performed his duties with great dignity and it was an added bonus that he was able to bring home food scraps. I remember having afternoon tea with them on the way home from school: Nescafé, black and unsweetened, served in tin mugs with ceremonial courtesy by the lady-in-waiting. The prince, a delicate blond boy, often walked along barefoot, with his one and only pair of shoes slung over his shoulder, to save them. I wore my father's brogues. Several sizes too big, with paper stuffed into the toes, they were not comfortable, but they were sturdy and made a change from my brown plastic sandals, which gave me blisters when I walked in them for longer distances.

I no longer fitted easily into the role of schoolgirl. Too much had happened. Most of what I was supposed to learn seemed totally irrelevant to the situation we were in. There was also the inner conflict of having to face the fact that almost everything I had sincerely believed in had been wrong, that my previous ideals had proved to be false. My family and I had been part of a regime that had brought death and terrible suffering to millions of people. Confronted with evidence of the atrocities that had occurred, I was shocked and deeply ashamed. When I looked back on all that my family had experienced, I felt hurt and betrayed because the ideology I had been brought up to accept as true and good had not turned out to be what I thought it was. It was almost impossible to reconcile the fact that my parents, whom I loved and respected and whom I know to have been honourable and caring people, could have been so involved in the Nazi regime that they had turned a blind eye to the many evil things that had been happening. I also failed to see, and still do, how and why I should be held personally responsible for things I did not do and events I could not possibly have influenced in any way.

There were teachers who resented having a 'Nazi brat' in their classes and took every chance to humiliate me. My classmates and I got on fine, often presenting a united front against repressive authority. We were a conglomeration of pupils from very diverse backgrounds. Apart from the locals, there were three ex-soldiers, one escapee from a Russian prison camp, one survivor from a German concentration camp and several refugees from the east.

One day there was a particularly virulent attack on me. Our Latin teacher got carried away lecturing on Caligula, one of the most unpleasant and murderous of the Roman emperors. He made me come forward and stand beside him, facing the class, then ordered me to repeat after him: 'General Höfle (my father) is the modern version of Caligula'. When I refused and tried to get away from him, back to my seat, he leapt in front of me and was about to grab my shoulders. This was the moment when someone from the back of the class threw a knife that missed the teacher and me but stuck fast in the blackboard behind us. The class was in uproar and the teacher fled out the door. By the time he returned, accompanied by the director, the knife had been removed and we were all sitting quietly in our seats, writing Latin exercises. The director had the good sense to keep his questioning to a minimum, since nobody in the class recalled an untoward incident involving a knife.

Apart from the family who had taken over my grandmother's estate, there were two distant relatives in a village not far from Augsburg. Frau Baas (Mrs Cousin), as she liked to be addressed, owned a bakery. She was a large woman with a big bosom restrained under a starched white apron, rusty brown hair in a bun, restrained under a hairnet, and hard eyes. She had agreed to give us some bread coupons every two months or so but she would make me wait in a corner of her shop for a long time, occasionally fixing a glittering eye on me. 'Come here,' she would finally hiss. 'Don't lose it, don't let anybody see it!' And with her red sausage-shaped fingers she would fish some coupons out of her till and put them into a small brown envelope which she slapped onto the counter. I always thanked her politely and closed the door of her shop gently so that the bell just tinkled, although I really felt like at least slamming the door or, better still, throwing the envelope back and poking my tongue out at her.

The other relatives who owned a butcher's shop were much kinder and their daughter was particularly friendly and understanding. I never had to ask. When I turned up at their house, they invited me into their kitchen and gave me a meal and a hefty parcel to take home. Once, in winter, I missed the evening train south from Munich that would have enabled me to get home that night, so I stayed in Munich, at Erika's place.

The next morning, very dark, very cold, very early, I set off to walk to the railway station. It was really too risky to be out of doors: it was only six o'clock and the curfew did not lift before seven. In Munich, under American occupation during the winter of 1945-46, it was not advisable for a girl of 16 to walk alone through the English Gardens at that hour. It was foolhardy and illegal and I was asking for it. I did not really consider what 'it' implied. I had to catch the seven twenty train south. There were no trams or buses running before seven; if I waited till then, there was no way I could make it to the railway station in time.

My mother had expected me home the evening before and I knew she would be frantic with worry. It had been a successful foray: my relatives had been generous, perhaps because I had handed over my father's signet ring as a gift. This time I was bringing home bacon. And not only that, there were four loaves of bread and a kilo of lard in the aluminium suitcase I carried. Some precious bread coupons were tucked into my bra. The side of bacon was securely strapped to my front, the extra girth hardly noticeable under my bulky winter coat, I hoped.

Hurrying along the snowy path, bordered by trees and bushes, I suddenly found my way blocked by two men who had silently and swiftly emerged from the undergrowth. Turning to run away from them, I was confronted by three more men. Now they encircled me. My heart was racing, but I also felt very cold, outwardly calm and determined to survive – with my bacon. So I stood absolutely still on that path and put my suitcase down on the snow, between my legs.

They were big men wearing fur hats, sheepskin coats and boots. They looked East European, were probably black marketeers, if not worse. One, who had a black moustache curving down over his mouth, spoke: 'Where you go, girl?'

'To the railway station.' Quivering, but defiant.

'Give the suitcase!'

'No.' This seemed to amuse him. 'What in suitcase?'

'Food. Bread and lard.'

'Show!' And so I bent down, undid the lock and opened it up, holding onto the case with hands and feet.

'You steal this?'

'No. I buy.' I was beginning to talk like them.

'On black market?'

'No. From aunt.'

They tittered, then said, 'You have money. Give money.'

I fished in my pocket and held out all the money I had, 20 marks – just enough for the train ticket. Moustache man took it, looked at it by the glow of his cigarette lighter, snorted and showed it to the others. There was more amusement and rapid talking. Although not understanding a word, I sensed a change for the better.

'Take money back.' Moustache man offered my 20 marks on his outstretched palm.

When I gingerly took it, he grasped my hand and held it firmly. 'What time train?' and, on my answer, 'Quick. We take you train. Not good alone.'

We galloped to the station, all six of us, one of them carrying my suitcase, moustache man and another bearded fellow dragging me between them, supporting me, saving me from stumbling. No time to buy the ticket. As we plunged through the gate the guard stepped aside smartly, not willing to argue with these five burly foreigners! The train was just starting to move as they manhandled me into the end carriage, threw my suitcase in after me and slammed the door. They stood on the platform, waving their arms, shouting something unintelligible, laughing and slapping each other on the shoulders. Their panting breath formed a cloud around them, almost like a halo. From the safety of the train, suitcase between my legs, I waved back, panting and laughing, with tears running down my cheeks.

CHAPTER 22

My Father

Fifty-four years after my father's death and I still can hardly bear to think about it. It requires an act of courage to read through the few letters and documents I have kept hidden for all this time. But I must do it now. Perhaps if I relive those times of anguish, bring the pain out into the open, I will resolve some of the issues that have lain so heavy on my heart.

We were notified by a letter from his solicitor that my father was to stand trial at the war tribunal at Nuremberg. Appointed by the tribunal, the solicitor was an earnest young man, well-meaning, sympathetic, just out of law school and no match for the American prosecutor. When my mother and I went to Nuremberg, hoping to see my father, the solicitor met us at the railway station and informed us that my father had not been indicted at Nuremberg, had not been accused of any war crimes, but that the Czechoslovakian Republic had requested his extradition and he had been sent to Bratislava a few days before. This was bad news indeed. We knew of the intense hatred the communist regimes of Eastern Europe had for all Germans.

We requested and were granted an interview with the American prosecutor, Mr Kempner. When we were ushered into his office, I felt instinctively that we could not expect any fairness or impartiality. He was our enemy. It was his intent to prosecute and punish all members of a regime he loathed and he would use all means at his disposal to achieve his aims. My mother asked on what charges my father had been extradited. 'Madam,' he replied, 'no charges as yet, but I am sure they will find something.'

My mother asked if there was any chance of my father being brought back to an internment camp in Germany.

'I'm not interested in having him brought back,' was the reply. 'There's no case to be answered at my court. I would only bring him back if you can guarantee that your husband will give evidence against his mates who are on trial here.'

My mother and I looked at each other. Her eyes were brimming. I had a big lump in my throat and found it hard to speak. 'He would never do that,' I croaked. My mother nodded.

There was a silence. 'Well, in that case ...'

My mother found her voice again. She whispered, 'There were two generals of the Czechoslovakian resistance movement. My husband saved their lives when they were caught. Perhaps they would speak for him now. Their names were General Golian and General Viest.'

Mr Kempner was suddenly very alert. 'I would very much like to find these two gentlemen. If you can tell me their whereabouts, I might consider a deal.'

We left, knowing it was hopeless. How could we find them? Perhaps they had perished in the last days of war. If they had survived and had risen to prominence under the new regime, would they risk their careers, their lives even, to help a former enemy who had once helped them? Unlikely. We went back to Kreuth, heavy-hearted.

Both Golian and Viest were professional soldiers, like my father. During the uprising in the Tatra in the autumn of 1944 they fought on opposite sides: they commanded the Partisan Slovak forces, my father the German forces in Slovakia. After some pretty fierce fighting, centred in the mountains near two villages in the middle part of Slovakia, Neusohl and Altsohl, the Germans won. At the end of October Banska Bystrica, the town at the centre of the uprising, fell. The Slovak State President, Josef Tiso, together with my father, accepted the surrender of the Partisan forces. Five thousand prisoners of war were taken. According to Slovak evidence, the German troops treated their opponents with fairness.

Generals Viest and Golian tried to make their way south, but they were betrayed and captured. According to an eye-witness, 'The Germans gave them each a cigarette and drove off with them in their car.' My father told me that he saw them as fellow soldiers, patriots of their country and opponents who had fought honourably and lost their battle. He shook hands with them at the moment of capture. My father was expected to hand both officers over to the Gestapo (German Secret State Police) but he knew their fate would be sealed if that happened and he felt he could not do that. He also knew, however, that he could not let them escape from his custody so he followed the only course compatible with his conscience: he arranged for both generals to be given civilian clothes, urged them not to reveal their identity to anyone and sent them as anonymous prisoners of war to be interned in a camp in Slovakia. His plan worked: they vanished without a trace.

When Himmler found out, he was furious. He sent a dispatch to my father, which ended with the words: 'Höfle, dass kann Dir den Kragen kosten'. (Höfle, that can cost you your neck.) But Himmler could not carry out his threat. My father was a close friend to two of the most influential Slovakians at the time, the State President, Josef Tiso, who was a Catholic priest, and the Bishop of Bratislava, Michael Buzalka. My father must have been popular, too, with a considerable faction of the Slovak people, at least with those who were anti-communist and anti-Czech, because Slovakia, with German encouragement, had become an autonomous state during the preceding years.

My father was awarded a prestigious order by the Slovak Republic. I have the lapel badge of it in my possession. On a red ribbon with two gold stripes is an eagle, wings outstretched, clasping two crossed swords in his claws. On the bird's body is a red shield showing a double cross. He was also presented with a car, the Tatra limousine, as a gift from the people of Slovakia.

On 9 December 1947 we received word that my father, together with Josef Tiso, had been sentenced to death by the tribunal at Bratislava. This was the first time my mother cried in front of us two girls. 'You must go to Nuremberg and make a plea for a pardon,' she told me. 'Go at once.'

I did not want to go. I knew in my heart that my father would not ask for pardon; it was not in his code of honour to do so. I also knew not to expect a sympathetic hearing from the American prosecutor at Nuremberg – he would not help the very people he saw as criminals. But I went.

The train for Munich and on to Nuremberg left within the hour. I was on it. I remember nothing of the journey, except that there was sleet and rain all day. When I arrived at Nuremberg railway station late in the afternoon, it was dark and gloomy. I rang my father's solicitor from a phone box. He sounded surprised and embarrassed but said he would meet me at the tram stop outside the station in 20 minutes, so I waited, for those long, cold 20 minutes.

'I'm very sorry,' he said when he came, 'your father was executed this morning. Very sorry. Please convey my sympathy to your mother and sister.' He shook my hand and was gone, boarding the tram that had stopped in front of us. I had to lean against the post of the tram stop for a while because my legs felt wobbly, my head fuzzy. The rain ran down my nose and my face was wet, but not from tears. I was too numb to cry.

Later I went back into the hall of the railway station and leaned against a pillar there. How long I stayed there I do not know, but it must have been quite late in the evening when a nun in a black habit approached me and laid her hand on my arm. 'I've seen you standing here for a long time,' she said. 'Where are you sleeping tonight?'

'I don't know.' I looked at her. Under the veil was a wrinkled face, a mouth that smiled kindly and a pair of very bright dark eyes.

'Then you must come with me, child,' she said encouragingly and firmly, so I obeyed. We went to the shelter for the homeless that her order had set up near the railway station. The shelter was full that night, all the beds occupied already, but she put up a camp stretcher for me next to the boiler down in the cellar. 'A warm place for you to sleep,' she said, tucking me into the grey blankets.

But I could not sleep. I could see my father, hear him say, 'I'm not ashamed of anything I've done. I'm not a criminal.' What had he been convicted of? How had he died? Did he suffer much? Was he brave to the end? I loved him. I could no longer tell him how much I loved him. I would never see him again. I hurt all over.

Early the next morning I sat in the nun's office. She made me eat the breakfast another sister had put on the desk in front of her. 'Nonsense,' she said when I refused at first, knowing it was her breakfast she now offered me: porridge and a mug of milky coffee. 'Do you know where you're going today?' she asked softly.

'I must go home and tell my mother that my father is dead.' Then the floodgates opened and I could not stop sobbing as I blurted out the whole story to her. If she was shocked, she did not show it. She just sat in her chair, listening quietly, then said, 'Yes, you must go home at once. I'll take you to your train.' She hugged me goodbye on the platform. 'God be with you,' she whispered as the train started to move. But God was a long way away.

I cannot remember anything of the journey back to Kreuth and I cannot remember how I told my mother and sister the news. But I can still see the three of us sitting in the front pew of St Leonard's, the old village church on the hill in Kreuth, the evening Father Engelmann conducted a memorial service for my father. The church was packed; the village remembered that he had prevented bloodshed and destruction on that day in May 1945. I can see the big wreath and the floral tributes on the steps to the altar, I can see the candles flickering, I can see the saints looking down on us from their pedestals, but there is no coffin. My father's body is not there.

The organ played and the congregation sang but I could not sing with them; my throat hurt too much. I still hurt all over, thinking of how lonely my father must have been during his last days, how he must have felt, going to his death. I was also thinking of how many others had died violent deaths, how many other bodies lay in places far from their loved ones, thinking how terribly sad, how awfully futile it was.

Why, then, was my father, Hermann Höfle, together with Josef Tiso and the German Ambassador Hans Ludin, executed in 1947? According to Dr Rasla, one of the chief prosecutors of the Slovakian Tribunal, it was a political act, the consequence of the post-war situation Slovakia found itself in as part of the Soviet-dominated eastern bloc. The new government of Slovakia, now reluctantly reunited with the Czech Republic, and much under influence of the communist powers, had to prove itself. It had to convince its own citizens as well as the Czechs that the new government had finished with fascism for once and for all and of its own volition. To achieve this, the National Council passed its own law to prosecute and punish those who had collaborated with Germany and the German authorities who had been in command. Josef Tiso, Hans Ludin and my father: three graves, side by side in a corner of the Bishop St Martinus cemetery in Bratislava, were all that remained.

After the collapse of the Soviet Empire, Slovakia gained independence and became a democratic state. Josef Tiso is once again popular, remembered and cherished as a national hero, and his grave has been relocated and is surrounded by floral tributes. When my son was in Bratislava in 1994, he wanted to visit his grandfather's grave but he was told by the authorities that the graves of my father and Hans Ludin could no longer be found.

Only now have I steeled myself to look again at the few documents that bear witness to the tragic events of 1947. There is the letter of Michael Buzalka, Bishop of Bratislava, who wrote in Latin to the parish priest of Kreuth, Father Engelmann. In the letter he asks Father to tell us 'in the kindest way' about the death of my father and asks that a mass be held in the village church in his memory. 'The so-called people's court sentenced General Höfle to death,' he wrote. 'He died on the 9th of December. Asked by the court for a last word, he called out: "Es lebe Deutschland!" (Long live Germany).'

On 8 December the highest official of the Czechoslovakian court granted my father's request for Bishop Buzalka to visit him in his cell to hear confession and give him communion. 'I want to be buried here in Slovakian soil to wait for the resurrection of the dead on the day of the Last Judgement. I do not accept the verdict of this court. It is unjust. I am not a criminal,' said my father. He asked the bishop to convey his heartfelt thanks to his dear wife and his daughters for the happiness and love he had been able to share with them. He asked his daughters Helga and Sigrid to always love and support their mother.

'My dearest Helga, Stay loving and honest. Support each other and always care for your dearest mother and Sigrid. You have always been my happiness and joy. Remain faithful to God. Know that I am beyond the stars, your adviser and protector forever. I salute you, my three loved ones and my country. I kiss you. I love you always. Your Dad.' That was his last letter, written on 8 December 1947.

His last photo stands before me on my desk. He sits with his elbows leaning on a plain table; a few writing implements lie in front of his folded hands. He looks very tired. He wears his uniform jacket, plain now, without the adornment of insignias and decorations. It hangs loose: he has lost weight in prison. His hair is receding and appears to be greying at the temples. When I look at his face, tears still fill my eyes. He looks so resigned, defeated. He is trying to smile, probably because he hopes that his family will receive the photo, but it is only a very small smile. It is a picture of a man who has lost his battle. A man who has lived and fought all his life for an ideology that proved to be false. A man who feels betrayed. He, who would lay down his life for his country without hesitation, who has believed its leader, has been faithful and honourable, true to his oath of allegiance, is now about to be executed, a scapegoat, a pawn in the game of political expediency. Yet I see no bitterness in his face. He has transcended the hurt and shame and regret and anger.

I know he had love for his family and country in his heart and that he believed in the goodness and power of God. I hope love and faith remained with him at the hour of his death and beyond.

CHAPTER 23

Munich after the War

In 1948 I left the Tegernsee high school before matriculation. Children of Nazis were not eligible to study at university in the immediate post-war years so there was no incentive to stay at school. I had wanted to study for a degree leading to journalism, but now explored my other interests, sculpting and painting. I had no great talent for either discipline, but liked 'making things'. Through friends of the old professor's wife I was recommended to and eventually apprenticed to a pottery studio at Bad Wiessee, a pretty little spa resort on the shores of Tegernsee.

I walked to and from work, one and a half hours each way, because I did not have money for the bus fare. I was not paid; it was considered lucky that I did not have to pay to be apprenticed. I swept the floor, put the clay slabs through the grinder, washed and stacked the shelves, pottied and fed my employers' baby, but never got near the potter's wheel or had any tuition. They felt that I was ungrateful when I told them that I was leaving after four months of unpaid labour. Apparently an apprentice was expected to be a general dogsbody for the first year, an unskilled labourer for the second and a learner for the third year, all at his or her own expense.

My second foray into the arts turned out to be equally disastrous. A local sculptor and painter took me on as his pupil, but this time the terms were different. He would teach me, free of charge, and I would model for him, under the supervision of his wife. My mother had misgivings, but I got my own way.

All went well for a while, he was a good teacher and I learned a lot about sculpting and sketching. The modelling was boring after I had overcome initial embarrassment. I had to 'keep the pose', remaining still for absolutely ages, while his wife supervised, sitting unobtrusively in a corner, knitting baby clothes for the expected second infant. It was all very decorous … until she, poor soul, got tired of this and supervised no more. The artist got amorous; I, impressionable and inexperienced, likewise. After a clandestine and unhappy affair lasting three months I left, this time to further my artistic career at a private academy in Munich. This establishment proved to be an utter sham. Fortunately I discovered this after attending for only a fortnight, before losing a semester's enrolment fees. Thus ended my career as artist. I only returned to clay modelling and painting many years later, as a relaxing hobby.

When I first shifted to Munich, it still bore the scars of the bombing raids. Many buildings were burnt-out skeletons or simply mounds of rubble. There was not enough of anything: food, clothes, shelter, money or jobs. There was still a black market with American cigarettes as a coveted commodity. Most people in the street looked pale and shabby; it seemed to take all their energy just to stay alive. On the tram, the conductor would sometimes have to shake his passengers awake when it was time for them to alight. Exhausted from lack of food, they simply fell asleep as soon as they sat down for a short while. And it all seemed so futile. They had fought and suffered through four and a half years of war, all in vain: they had been defeated. They had been betrayed and abandoned by their government. The leaders they had believed in had been tried and found guilty of war crimes. There was dejection, there was shame, there was anger.

There was also the very real fear of communism, of the Soviet giant taking over Europe, as it had already swallowed Eastern Europe and half of Germany. It took a lot of determination and courage for the German people to start rebuilding their shattered lives. Apart from coping with the emotional trauma, they were dealing with the dramatic change of living under foreign occupation as a defeated nation. The economic infrastructure had been destroyed. Most industrial plants had either been bombed or dismantled as part of reparation payments. The transport system was severely damaged. There were no social services.

There were many foreign refugees, called displaced persons by the Allies, in West Germany. Most of them did not want to return to their Eastern European homelands where they faced annihilation. The Soviets showed no mercy to the dissidents they captured. Many displaced persons who had been forcibly repatriated were executed as soon as they crossed the border. There were also many refugees from East Germany and German ethnic minorities from countries now under Soviet rule. There were the thousands of people who had been ausgebombt (bombed out) and had lost their homes and all their possessions during the war. There were the German ex-prisoners of war, many searching for their families, who had become refugees.

There was not enough of anything we take for granted in a civilised society; there were too many disillusioned, hungry, dispossessed, desperate people. It was a scenario for chaos and political disaster only. When the Western Allies became aware of this, they saw to it that conditions gradually improved. The Marshall Plan enabled the economy to take heart. The Lord Mayor of Cologne, Konrad Adenauer, who became chancellor in 1949, proved to be a man of integrity, respected by the Allies and trusted by the German people. The fledgling Bundesrepublik (Federal Republic) took its first faltering steps towards economic recovery and political stability.

I had found accommodation for myself on the outskirts of Munich – in a cellar. I had my own entrance, so I could come and go as I pleased. The fact that 'my flat' consisted of one narrow damp room and had no facilities I took in my stride. I washed in my landlady's laundry tub, also in the cellar, used her toilet upstairs when in extreme need and made do with a one-bar heater and an electric jug for warmth and sustenance. There was little money to buy food that had to be cooked anyway so I lived mainly on bread, cheese and apples. The accommodation cost 10 marks a week. My landlady, a widow with a handicapped son, was a bit slapdash as far as cleanliness was concerned, but she took a kindly interest in my progress and occasionally invited me to share her meal. I learned to ignore her less than immaculate dinnerware and never to analyse the ingredients of her soups and stews.

It was during those first months in Munich that a good friend of my mother invited me to an MRA (Moral Rearmament) meeting. In post-war Germany many people existed in a vacuum; they were searching for ideas and ideals that would bring new hope and meaning to their lives. The MRA movement, founded in 1938 by American evangelist Frank Buchman, who had earlier established the Oxford Group, attracted people of diverse backgrounds, because it preached a simple message, based on the Sermon of the Mount. The 'Four Absolutes' – Absolute Honesty, Purity, Unselfishness and Love – were perceived as a foundation for a dynamic new lifestyle. The quiet time, when one reflected, gained insight and asked for guidance from above, was a form of spiritual discipline flexible enough to accommodate both those who were affiliated to a church and those who were not.

I was very impressed by the MRA philosophy and tried to adhere to it. The absolute honesty, unselfishness and love were hard but not impossible to aspire to, but I had great trouble with the absolute forgiveness: I could not reconcile this with my ideas about justice. But at one of the MRA rallies I was suddenly overcome by emotion and the strong urge to stand up and proclaim, 'I forgive the people who killed my father.' Tears were streaming down my face and I had to hold onto the back of the chair in front of me to stop my trembling. Blurred impressions of a general commotion came to a halt when I felt firm and kindly arms around my shoulders. They belonged to an elderly woman who moved forward to stand beside me. She took my hand and her voice rang out, 'I am Jewish and I have suffered. I forgive the people who caused my pain and anguish.'

Vally had lost many members of her family. She had survived by hiding for months in the underground railway system of Berlin until she was rescued by a Lutheran minister who organised for her care by a network of parishioners. So as not to endanger her hosts, she could never stay with one family for more than a few weeks before moving on. Vally was a woman of strength, wisdom and great inner beauty and she became a dear friend. She painted delicate watercolour landscapes and floral arrangements. We spent many sun-filled hours together, painting and talking, until she unexpectedly died in her sleep. She enriched my thinking and I remember her with love and gratitude.

My active involvement with the MRA movement gradually ground to a halt, for two reasons. I became disenchanted when I perceived manipulations by a hierarchy of those with political ambitions. But the more compelling reason was that I realised how easily I could be swept up into becoming an eager follower of a seemingly idealistic movement – just like my parents, who had made an enthusiastic commitment to National Socialism when it seemed to be an ideal worth following.

That my career then took a different direction, I owe to my good friend Hans, a secretary of the YMCA/YWCA (Young Men's and Women's Christian Association), who invited me to take part in the work he was doing for various refugee groups living in and around Munich. As only a true and unselfish friend would do, he initially paid me half his salary to share in his work with displaced persons. Hans devoted his life to refugees, in Germany during the post-war years and later in the United States, where he became a Presbyterian minister. Our friendship has lasted to this day. Much to our delight, he and his charming wife visited my husband Nick and me a few years ago and we were able to recount many memories of the interesting and turbulent times we had shared in Munich.

One of my early assignments in refugee work was to be counsellor at a summer camp for children. This was set up at a lakeside hotel at Prien, on the shores of the Chiemsee, and catered for groups of 80 to 100 children for periods of three weeks. The youngsters, aged between eight and 16, were of different nationalities, different backgrounds, different abilities, and they spoke different languages. They had only two things in common: they had survived horrific experiences and they did not know where their parents were, or if they still had parents. Many did not know their surname. The Red Cross had gathered them from roadsides, from bomb sites, from camps or from US army units, where they had latched on as 'mascots'. Some of them had banded together and lived in juvenile gangs; some had formed fiercely patriotic national groups.

Several were hyperactive and aggressive; others were withdrawn and passive, hardly responding to anything offered. All had their phobias. The first group of 12 and I slept on camp stretchers set up in a large attic room of the old hotel. We became very close on the third night, during a thunderstorm. I had trouble tucking them all into their blankets and was just dozing off myself, when the rumble of thunder and flashes of lightning caused hysteria and panic, the thunderclaps reminding them of gunfire. They screamed, they sobbed, they needed calming and comforting. We ended up, all 13 of us, in, under, on top and beside my camp stretcher, clinging hotly to each other with blankets over our heads so that we did not see the lightning.

They were well provided for at the summer camp: there was good wholesome food in great quantities, all they could possibly eat at mealtimes. But one of my group, a little boy of nine, always snatched anything left on the table and stuffed it down the front of his shirt. He never managed to eat his loot before the next meal and so he hid it in secret caches under the shrubs outside or in dark corners within the building. Poor wee fellow, he had been hungry so often that he wanted to be sure of his next meal. Another small boy had a wicked-looking knife strapped to his side. He would not give it up for anything, but thankfully did not attack anybody with it either. We overcame our language difficulties somehow, often by mime or sound effects. When one of my children, a delicate-looking Czech girl, flung herself into my arms, sobbing, I could not understand what had happened to her until she screamed, 'Bzzz me ow!' A bee had stung her. She happened to be one of the fortunate children: she remembered her surname and her father, a lawyer from Prague, traced her through the Red Cross. Great was the joy when her parents came to the summer camp to claim her.

The youngsters paddled and swam in the lake, always two by two. They had to hold up their arms, hands clasped with their partner's, whenever we blew a whistle. It worked well; nobody ever got into difficulties. We did crafts and sang, learned folk dancing, played games. One of their favourites was 'Raid', a cowboy and Indian type of game, which entailed storming a fort and sneaking through a line of defenders. Each child had a 'soul', a piece of red or blue wool tied around their wrist. If an opponent ripped off its soul, the child was a casualty and had to return to base. The game, played in the evenings on the wooded hill behind the hotel, was marked by much vigour and yelling, and we counsellors had a busy time arbitrating and ensuring that the playing did not become too realistic.

One night, when tallying up our cowboys and Indians, we found that 'my' Hungarian child, a girl of 15, and a 16-year-old Yugoslav boy who was the 'child' of our Estonian sports master, were missing. He and I trudged up the hill straightaway, searching, swinging our torches, shouting. I went to the left, he to the right. When we met again, on the top of the hill, I was frantic, calling loudly for 'my child'. The sports master took my elbow firmly and said, 'I saw them. She's not a child any more. Leave them be. They'll return in good time.' They did too, hand in hand and starry-eyed. I was glad I had followed the advice. My Hungarian girl died of lung cancer when she was 17; at least she had experienced a little happiness in her short life.

I became secretary of the International YM/YWCA Students' Association in Munich, which solved my financial problem as I was now paid a modest salary. The association had established a Mensa (Latin for table) for a group of about 200 students. This provided good meals at very reasonable cost and, as most students lived under harsh conditions with minimal funds at their disposal, the Mensa soon became the focal point for creature comforts and, most important, a place for making friends and sharing ideas.

Most of the students who belonged to the International YM/YWCA were enrolled at the various faculties and institutes of Munich University. Displaced persons from every nationality of central and eastern Europe, they all were keen to get the qualifications needed to begin a new life. Most of them wanted to emigrate to the 'new countries', the United States, Canada, Australia; a few went to Israel. Not one of them wanted to return to the countries from which they had been deported or had fled. In spite of our diverse national and political backgrounds, we soon became a close-knit group, supporting each other, having fun, engaging in lively debates on political or ethical topics, eating together. Many of the friendships made then have lasted to this day and one special person I met at the 'Y' became my husband.

The Mensa was situated in the basement of a bombed-out building, close to the university. We whitewashed the walls and on the ceiling painted a circle of the flags of each nationality represented in our group. Long wooden trestle tables and benches and a notice board completed the decor. From the kitchen, behind sliding doors at one end of the room, the meals were served on metal trays donated by the US Army. We employed a succession of cooks, recruited from the displaced persons' camps around Munich. They produced superb food, usually rather spicy and characteristic of whichever country they came from. Sadly, though, our cooks never stayed with us for long. The good ones found employment at much better pay at 'proper' restaurants and hotels; the dishonest ones pilfered and had to be dismissed. Some were afflicted with the bad temper so often associated with the creative talent of an inspired cook. We had to sack the pair who, in the heat of an argument, chased each other across the tabletops, one swinging a meat cleaver, the other a large carving knife.

I shifted from my cellar room into an apartment in München-Schwabing, not far from the university and the Mensa. An improvement in living conditions! I now had a room on the second floor of a big apartment building, with a large window overlooking a grassy square with the grand name of Kaiserplatz. Although the room was carpeted and furnished, I could not really make much use of the furniture since it consisted of a grand piano and a stack of three or four large leather-bound volumes of the Bible – antique treasures no doubt, but of little practical use to me. The apartment had a proper toilet, a bathroom where one could have a hot bath if the gas heater was fed enough 10 pfennig coins to spurt near-boiling water, and a kitchen, equipped with a gas range, also coin-operated, a sink and some shelves.

There were six rooms. The one to my right was occupied by a young architect and her partner. In the room to my left lived our landlady who was in her forties, single, very pious and with a passion for cakes. She collected our rent. When the electricity department cut off power and gas to the apartment, we tenants found, to our dismay, that she had spent all the rent money in her favourite café which she patronised daily. Across the hall from my room two male tailors lived in harmonious homosexual bliss – until the morning of my wedding, when they had a terrible disagreement. Alarmed by an ever-increasing volume of sobs, shouts and shrieks, which culminated in 'Don't kill me!', my brave husband-to-be sprinted across, wrenched open their door and wrestled a large carving knife away from the avenging tailor who had been deceived by his unfaithful partner.

There were two rooms along the corridor to kitchen and facilities. One was occupied by an elderly lady with a pungent smell who tapped her way around using a white cane; she said she was blind. She had our sympathy and we overlooked the fact that she pilfered food items left unattended for a few minutes in the kitchen. But one day I saw her picking up some coffee beans which had spilled onto the terrazzo floor of the kitchen. Her eyesight must have improved dramatically on that occasion.

In the other room lived a very shy and reclusive gentleman. On the rare occasions when we came upon him as he flitted to or from the kitchen or bathroom we had only a glimpse of a podgy figure with a shock of wavy black hair, large dark eyes behind thick glasses and a prominent nose. It seemed to upset him to come across the other tenants: he bolted back into his room, locking the door behind him. He was a writer, our landlady had told us. He probably wrote thrillers and was haunted by his creations.

CHAPTER 24

The Kalmucks

When working as a secretary of the YM/YWCA I often went into the displaced persons' camps just outside Munich. In one of these, an old army barracks, lived the Kalmucks. There were only 300 of them, wanted by nobody, the remnants of a minority, a lost tribe. They had roamed the steppes around the Black Sea since time began, fiercely proud and independent, governed only by the cycle of seasons and the availability of pasture for their herds of Karakul sheep, goats and horses.

Ah, their horses! Small and sinewy, with long flowing manes and tails and tough hooves, they had speed and stamina. They ranged free and wild, but the mares had the generosity of heart to let themselves be milked and the stallions would gently carry the smallest child atop bundles of bedding or pull the pole-sledges when it was time to pack up the yurts and search for fresh green grass. To say that the Kalmucks loved their horses would be an understatement. Their eyes shone when they spoke of their horses; they had been an essential part of their life and history. A Kalmuck and his horse were a single entity, moving, breathing, thinking as one.

Had they not been of Genghis Khan's Golden Horde? Riding, glorious, victorious and unstoppable, right into the heart of Europe. They had been conquerors in this land then and here they were again, but not as conquerors. This time they were fenced in, living – no, existing – in barracks, bereft of their horses, their livestock, their yurts, their freedom, their raison d'être.

They were displaced persons in Germany, a country that had more than enough dispossessed people of its own to want or care for this lost tribe of nomads, although they had fought on the German side against the Soviets, welcoming the German army when they had first met near the shores of the Black Sea. They saw the soldiers as allies in the fight against the hated oppres-

sor, the Soviets, who had taken away their freedom and threatened their ancient rights and customs. The Kalmucks were good fighters: it was in their
blood and the hardships of war were akin to the hardships of survival in the
steppes. As always, their families were with them when they fought and when
they moved.

When the German Army was in retreat to the west, the Kalmucks followed,
with their families, some of their old folk, sheep, goats and, of course, the
horses. Decimated by incredible suffering on the long trek, the pitiful remnants of the tribe, carrying a few tattered bundles and a few children on their
backs, ended up in Munich. The IRO (International Refugee Organisation),
now in charge of them, had 'settled' them in the wooden barracks of an obso-
lete army installation, surrounded by a high wire fence and far out of town.
They were lucky to be alive.

They were also a problem. What do you do with a bunch of nomads, alien
with their Asiatic looks and customs, unskilled in Western know-how and therefore unemployable, not suitable for emigration. They were unwilling to go
home, because there was no longer any place they could call home and if they
were repatriated by force, concentration camps and certain death would be
their fate. You could feed them, clothe them, contain them and leave them to
their own devices, hoping that sooner or later divine providence, in whatever
form, would intervene to find a solution. As it happened, they were followers
of the Dalai Lama. They were in spiritual contact with him, they said, spinning
their prayer wheels and chanting as they sat in a circle on the floor of the
dimly lit barracks. But the Dalai Lama was far away.

'There's been some trouble at the Kalmuck camp. Do you want to come
with me and see?' said the IRO official. I was fascinated by these people. The
trouble had been resolved when we got there and nobody had been killed,
this time. It had started when one of the young men had insulted the honour
of a young woman and she and her family wanted revenge. According to custom the elders decided that redress was called for, that justice had to be seen
and done. Two stout pegs were hammered into the hard earth of the former
parade ground and two leather thongs were attached, one short, one long. The
offender was tied by the ankle to the short thong, the avenger of the girl's
honour to the longer thong. Both men, stripped to the waist, were armed with
plaited stock whips, which they handled with deadly accuracy. The whole tribe,
in a wide circle around the combatants, watched in silence, waiting for the
raised hand, the signal from the aggrieved family to end the duel. Justice had

to be done. Had they decided that the culprit deserved death, the hand would not have been raised. Barbaric? Maybe. It depends how one looks at it.

Duelling with whips was regarded as an honourable fight. The culprit, although handicapped, had the chance to defend himself and everybody witnessed justice being done. The crime rate among the Kalmucks was very low indeed and reoffending was unheard of. When we arrived they all stood close together in the parade ground. Brown, flat, round faces. Black inscrutable eyes. Silent, even the few children. The replies to the interpreter's questions were dignified and impassive. No, there was no trouble. The dispute had been resolved. No, there had not been a murder. There was no need for an inquiry.

But there was a need for something to be done for the Kalmucks: integrate them somehow into Western society, teach them English, teach them German, give them skills for employment … As part of the education programme, the 'Y' took young Kalmucks out of the barracks, to join other youngsters of different nationalities at a 10-day summer camp on the shores of a secluded Bavarian lake. About 80 young Czechs, Poles, Yugoslavs, Hungarians, Ukrainians, Russians, boys and girls between 14 and 20, met there with 16 of 'my' Kalmucks, 12 boys and four girls. Shy at first, they soon joined in all the camp activities, although always as a group. The girls, always, wearing their long high-waisted dresses, dabbled dainty toes in shallow water, giggled, watched the others splash and swim, but refused to go in themselves.

The boys held their own in sports and excelled in archery, and in dancing. On campfire night each national group sang and danced their items, spirited or sad, eloquent in feeling, telling of their identity, pride and homesickness. Each group's item, though unique, was predictable, but not so the Kalmucks'. Theirs was no mere item, it was a storm from the steppes swooping around, over, through our campfire. They swirled, they leapt, they screamed, they danced to drums beating faster and faster. They were not boys any more, but warriors from the Golden Horde.

The audience, their spines tingling, were spellbound, grateful that Kalmucks' 'swords' were only sticks. I was even more grateful for the no weapons rule when they confided later, after the campfire had been doused and everybody was safely tucked into their tents, that the only thing missing from an otherwise perfect evening was that they had not been able to burn somebody at the stake, preferably a Russian!

On United Nations Day, 24 October, in 1949 the YM/YWCA decided to celebrate in a big way. Displaced persons of 17 nationalities, living in and around Munich, were invited to perform at the Amerika Haus in a prestigious event to which everybody who was anybody had been invited, including the Lord Mayor of Munich and the editor of *Neue Zeitung*, the American Edgar Jamieson, famous for setting up Bavaria's first post-war 'democratic and unbiased' newspaper.

Again the Kalmucks stole the show, but this time it was the women who captivated the audience. Row upon row they floated onto the stage, wearing floor-length dresses in bright hues of red, yellow, orange and green. Gracefully moving and intertwining their wide-sleeved arms, they glided and hovered like butterflies, sometimes fast, sometimes slow, weaving intricate patterns to the beat of muted drums. Their iridescent bodies topped by completely quiet faces, unsmiling, their eyes closed to mere slits, they belonged to a calm and inaccessible realm, separated from us as if behind a wall of glass. They remained impassive and remote, even when the audience gave them a standing ovation.

'Eat with us,' they had said when I visited their barracks one day and I felt honoured at the invitation. There were no tables or chairs, so we all sat on camp stretchers. Bowls, filled from a big cauldron with a very hot and very spicy stew, were passed around. There was much bowing, slurping and belching during the meal, as demanded by Kalmuck etiquette, signalling that the food was good and appreciated. My mouth on fire as I ate cabbage, black beans, chilli peppers and some lumps of meat, I slurped and belched with the best of them. 'Is good?' 'Is very good.' We were friends. I was told later that I had eaten dogmeat.

What became of the Kalmucks? Some of the young men found employment with Zirkus Krone, Munich's resident circus, where they performed an act called 'Indian Attack', which involved bareback riding, much cracking of whips and knife throwing. It made me sad to watch, but they seemed happy. A group of 50 or so went to Texas to look after free-ranging Angora goats, and Sancha, one of their young chiefs, studied in Germany and became an engineer, but as for the others, I do not know. The time had come for me to leave and journey to the other end of the earth.

CHAPTER 25

Nick

Nick, Nikolaj Nikolajvich, my Russian husband, worked as administration officer for the IRO in an office just outside Munich, near the refugee camp at Schleissheim, where he and his parents lived. How they got there is a long story that would fill a volume by itself.

In short, the family had been landed gentry, farming a large property in the eastern region of the Ukraine, near Donesk. Fiercely anti-Bolshevik and loyal to the Tsar, Nick's father, Nikolaj Jaklevich had been an officer in the White Russian Army (the Whites fought the Reds or Bolsheviks). In 1918, to evade capture, he fled to Turkey, where he and many fellow officers were interned. When France offered asylum to White Russians, he and his fellow officers were transported to their destination by train through the Balkans and Czechoslovakia. Nikolaj Jaklevich stepped off the train at Prague, because he felt he would rather live in a Slavic environment, more akin to his beloved Russia.

He studied in Prague, became a surveyor and by 1924 he had saved enough money to buy his wife, Jekaterina Wassilievna, and child from the Soviets. They joined him to live in Munkachevo, a small town near the Hungarian border. Nick, his son, was six years old when he first met his father.

At eight, the little boy was bundled off to a Russian boarding school 1000 kilometres away in Mährisch-Trübau, to be educated and indoctrinated in the traditional manner of Holy Russia. The ex-generals and professors teaching there did a thorough job: to this day, more than 70 years later, Nick still adheres to the ideas implanted so long ago. The family lived in Czechoslovakia until 1945, when they once again had to flee from the Soviets, this time to Germany.

Nick came into my office one day in the autumn of 1949, delivering cartons of books that had been donated to our students' group by the IRO. He

The last photograph I have of my father, taken in December 1947. He wears his uniform jacket, plain now, without the adornment of insignias and decorations. He is trying to smile, probably because he hopes that his family will receive the photo, but it is only a very small smile. It is a picture of a man who has lost his battle.

Helene became the proud mother of a fine son after the war had ended.

LEFT: My mother, in the early 1950s.

Erika, in a photo taken after the war.

Inge, my best friend in Bad Harsburg.

Vally

My office at the YMCA was in the old Air Ministry, the building in front of which Erika and I had shaken Hitler's hand.

With friends in Munich.

A great mixture of nationalities worked at the YMCA – here in one photo are Canadian, Rumanian, British, Russian, German and Hungarian representatives.

The Mensa in Munich.

With my good friend Hans.

Nick, my soon-to-be husband!

says he knew, the minute he saw me, 'That's the girl I'm going to marry.' I cannot remember love at first sight, but recall that I thought him charming, gentle and good-looking. When Nick joined the students' group, we met almost daily and a friendship developed that led to romance.

We became engaged on Easter Saturday 1950 at Meersburg, Lake Constance, where we were attending a conference with about 20 of our student friends. On a stroll through Meersburg we saw a ring we liked in a small jeweller's shop. In Germany, it is the custom to have gold bands only as engagement rings for both partners – no diamonds. The ring is worn on the left hand until the wedding day, when the date and name of the partner is engraved on the inside of the ring, which is then worn on the right hand. The jeweller had only one ring available, but when he saw how disappointed we were, he promised to make another that same day. He was as good as his word and we celebrated our engagement in the circle of our friends at the breakfast table at the conference centre. Nick and I then went to Kreuth, where he, with all due formality, asked my mother for my hand in marriage. My mother and sister had met Nick before, of course, and liked him, but it had not occurred to them that our relationship was serious enough for us to contemplate marriage. To tell the truth, I had not considered marriage either: I seemed just to sail right into it, without giving much thought as to the consequences.

Anyway, my mother said yes and we were married on 11 June 1950. I was 20, Nick 11 years older. Some of mother's friends were shocked at the idea of my marrying a Russian. Dear old Aunt Agatha took me aside and whispered, 'Do you really have to do this? A Russian of all people!' I told her that I did not have to but wanted to marry Nick. She was gracious enough to give us three of her heirloom silver spoons as a wedding gift. Aunt Agatha also had grave misgivings when we emigrated to New Zealand the following year. 'So dangerous with all those cannibals running around,' she wailed. When, many years later, I was visiting Germany and she saw me using cutlery in the correct order at a formal dinner party, she nodded approval. 'I'm so glad that you have not forgotten how to use a knife and fork.' I replied that we sometimes ate at the table in New Zealand, although we usually just tore meat from bone with teeth and fingers, crouching around a campfire in the bush with our cannibal friends. She did not quite know how to take this.

We were married twice. The first marriage ceremony, at the registrar's office, as required by German law, took about 10 minutes. It was all very official and slick, we emerged clutching our Heiratsurkunde (marriage certificate), duly witnessed by four staunch friends. The second marriage ceremony, in a Russian Orthodox church, was much more meaningful and memorable. There was much emotion, much singing, much chanting and much incense. Six of our friends took turns holding two golden crowns above our heads during the lengthy exchange of vows, which had to be voiced in Russian and German. Before the Orthodox priest, our good friend Father Benningson, slid the wedding rings on our right hands, we both had to step onto a white mat. It is customary for the groom to step onto the mat first, meekly followed by his bride, thus symbolising the authority of husband over wife. This was one custom I did not subscribe to: we stepped onto that mat together!

The little church could not hold the large contingent of friends who came to wish us well and we ran out of food at the party held later that afternoon at the Mensa. My mother, always resourceful, rolled up her sleeves and went into the kitchen to produce mountains of sandwiches to feed the ever-increasing throng. It was a very happy and hilarious party, even if there was only one glass of bubbly each for those guests astute enough to arrive in time for the toast. Nick's mother attended the church service but his father did not come to the wedding. Only years later did I realise the extent of their disapproval of their only son's choice of a non-Russian, non-Orthodox marriage partner.

After a brief honeymoon, spent in Bad Harzburg at my dear friend Inge's invitation, we settled down to married bliss in our one-room flat, each working at our respective jobs. My culinary skills improved. Two dishes were perfected to dinner party standard – spaghetti bolognese and filled tomatoes with potato purée – and with this repertoire at my fingertips, we entertained. One frequent and very welcome guest was Father Benningson. A striking bearded figure with shoulder-length hair and wearing flowing black robes, he usually carried a small, black, official-looking case. This, one would suppose, contained the sacraments, or oil for extreme unction. Not so. The question and answer game we played at his arrival was always the same: 'What do you think I have in this case, my children?' We had to reply that we had no idea. Much to our surprise and delight he would then extract a bottle of brandy or vodka. 'Spiritual comfort,' he called it.

Our circle of friends was drawn from the international, inter-denominational, inter-racial spectrum of the population in post-war Munich. A colourful, wonderful pot-pourri of friends! Fate had thrown us all together, a volatile mixture of personalities who overcame their differences to become a close-knit, supportive and caring group. There was Hans, my special friend and mentor, who started the International YM/YWCA Students' Association in Munich. There was Don, the American Baptist minister who, after serving in Munich, went on with his wife Mary to help refugees in Lebanon and several African republics for many years before finally settling in rural England. There was Janos the Rumanian officer who had belonged to the Iron Guard. He disappeared behind the Iron Curtain, in his words, to 'attend to unfinished business'. There was Ruth, the Black American Quaker who, with her professor husband, later settled in the Virgin Islands. Kolja, formerly an officer in the Soviet Army, who became a successful lecturer and business man in the United States, is still a close friend, as is Ursula, the Polish intellectual who emigrated to the States, married an Italian and raised a family in New York. There were the charming Armenians, Antaram and her brother Gugas, who managed to get their aged parents out to settle with them in New York.

There was inscrutable Poluski, also Polish, who sadly hanged himself when his activities as a double agent became unbearable. There was Joshka, the Hungarian officer, and Anna, the aristocratic Russian, pianist, and Hermänle, the Jewish student, who offered to tattoo my left arm with a concentration camp number to facilitate my immigration to the United States: 'Hardly any pain and I will say I saw you there and you will say you saw me'. There was Fred, the German student, delightfully gay and a staunch friend for a girl to have. One Bulgarian lass, Dantsche, went a bit wild, having escaped from purdah (the Islamic behaviour code for women). During a heated political discussion, Leonid, the fiercely patriotic Ukrainian, had to be restrained from strangling his opponent. Fedor, Professor of Russian Literature at Munich University, was patron of our group, a godfather-like figure. There was Herb, the American journalist, who tore up his American passport and declared himself to be a 'world citizen'. There were several German journalists, as well as members of Munich's intellectual set, the MRA contingent and a sprinkling of IRO officials. Our discussions on topical and historical matters were more than lively!

CHAPTER 26

Emigration

Nick and I had been married for just one year. We continued to work and live in Munich and Nick's parents were still living in the refugee camp at Schleissheim, just outside the city. They were anxious to emigrate to the United States, where relatives who had already settled there were willing to guarantee initial accommodation and employment, and, of course, wanted their only son to go with them. But his marriage to me, a German citizen, stymied their plans. They could have emigrated almost immediately under the Russian quota, but the German quota for immigration was filled and that meant an indefinite wait and worry for them; they wanted to get out of a country that was so perilously close to the Soviet threat. Now I can understand their frustration and anger about our marriage, but at the time I failed to recognise this as a reason for their antipathy towards me.

It must have been a dilemma for Nick to juggle his love for his parents and his love for me. He, too, wanted to emigrate. There seemed to be little prospect, in the foreseeable future, of finding suitable employment in his profession as civil engineer in Germany and the start of the Korean War made the possibility of the Cold War in Europe escalating a worry.

In June 1951 a happy solution presented itself, out of the blue. In conversation with a Hungarian doctor, Nick learned that an Australian and New Zealand mission was in Munich to select immigrants for their respective countries. 'But it's too late for you to apply,' the doctor told him. 'Applications have closed.' At that moment, Nick says, he knew he wanted to emigrate to New Zealand and was certain he would succeed. The same day he managed to wangle an appointment with the New Zealand officials. I was startled when he hurtled into my office, excited and happy, shouting, 'Quick, get into the jeep, we're going for an interview with the New Zealand mission.'

The mission consisted of three official and serious-looking gentlemen sitting behind a long table that was strewn with files and documents. They surveyed us, unsmiling and stern. I wondered what New Zealand was like, where exactly it was. Somewhere in the Pacific Ocean? But the Pacific was so big and so far away. Were New Zealanders a stern and unsmiling people? Through my mind flitted images of dour missionaries who expected one to conform to their beliefs and standards. I felt uneasy.

Nick nudged me, urgently. They had asked a question and I was required to respond.

'So you want to emigrate to New Zealand?' one of the officials said. 'New Zealand is a pioneering country. Are you aware of that?'

Nick and I nodded. I tried to appear eager.

'You will have to live and work as directed by the New Zealand government for the first two years in our country. Do any work required – manual work, pioneering work. Are you prepared for that?'

I had visions of living in a little hut in dense jungle. I must have looked a trifle doubtful, because the next question was directed at me by the oldest and sternest-looking missionary. 'Are you prepared to do pioneering work?'

'Like what?' I asked cautiously. 'Like felling trees?'

'Yes,' he replied, with perhaps just a hint of a smile.

'If they were little trees, I could,' I said and knew that this was the correct answer and that Nick was pleased with me.

'Very well, your application will be processed and you'll be notified soon.' We were dismissed.

'Soon' was very soon indeed: we were accepted and within a fortnight we were on our way. I hardly had time to find the location of New Zealand in an atlas. It looked very small, very far away. New Zealand was one of only a few countries accepting elderly immigrants as part of a family group, so Nick's parents were accepted with us, although they were both in their sixties. They were not at all pleased about going to New Zealand instead of the United States, but Nick was determined. He knew in his heart that this was the country for us and he was right.

My mother was very brave about my going to the other end of the earth; not once did she voice her heartache. She did all she could with limited funds and the short time available to equip us for this adventurous undertaking, even to the extent of procuring two pith helmets. Neither she nor I fully realised at the time of parting just how far away I was going and that I would live there forever. Only when I saw my mother again, 12 years later, when she was at the end of her life, did she say that my distance from her hurt like an open wound which never healed. Only now do I understand that I failed to carry out my father's last wish. He had asked me to always look after my mother and four years after his death I settled on the other side of the world, leaving my sister with the responsibility of caring for my mother. Not fulfilling my obligation is the only regret I have about settling in New Zealand.

My mother, Sigrid and I kept in close contact by frequent letters of course, but we missed the special joy of a hug, the immediacy of sharing a laugh or a tear. They had to cope with their problems, I had to cope with mine – we were so far apart. Although life was not easy for them during the first few years after my departure, their financial situation gradually improved and my mother built a modest house in Kreuth. Always supported by my sister and a host of good friends, she enjoyed her walks in the mountains, taking part in village life, and the company of her dogs.

She was very happy about the arrival of our son, Michael, and would have loved to get to know him and her two granddaughters, Sonja and Katerina, but this was not to be. In 1960, after the arrival of our daughter Sonja, she and we had saved enough for her to visit us in Stratford, but two weeks before she was to depart she had to undergo emergency surgery for cancer of the stomach. She seemed to make a good recovery and we made plans for another visit, this time to Te Kuiti, where we had moved when Sonja was still a baby. But early in March 1963 my mother was rushed to hospital again with cancer of the liver. It was terminal; she died in June.

I had not foreseen just how drastic the consequences of marrying Nick were, how they would change my life forever. We loved each other and we wanted to build a future together, but I had never thought that this future would mean leaving behind all I loved, embarking on a journey into the unknown, becoming a displaced person myself. Perhaps it was as well that our departure to New Zealand happened so swiftly, irrevocably. Before I had time for second thoughts, I became an infinitesimal part of the mass of people who were emigrating all over the globe, one of the numbers of displaced persons destined for shipment to New Zealand.

CHAPTER 27

Number 169

I was labelled 169 and that number replaced the person I used to be. It was also stamped on my meagre belongings, which consisted of a metal box and a battered suitcase. As a dependant – appendage? – of her new husband and his parents, 169 had become one of the contingent of 500 or so refugees who embarked on the journey to New Zealand. It was a country 169 knew nothing about, apart from its geographical position. She did not realise just how far away this was, how permanent would be the separation from her old identity, her family, her roots. She only knew that she loved her new husband, that she had promised to go wherever he went, like Ruth in the Bible, and that he was convinced New Zealand was the best place to emigrate to.

Of the 10-hour train journey from Munich to Naples 169 remembers little, except going over the Brenner Pass, where tall larches moved their branches gracefully, like ballerinas dancing in the evening wind. Through the night the train rattled south, to Bagnoli transit camp near Naples. Formerly the barracks where El Duce had trained his troops for the African campaign, by 1951 Bagnoli was the IRO transit camp for displaced persons on their way to Australia and New Zealand.

At Bagnoli 169 stood in long queues, waiting to be inoculated, fed, allocated a bunk, drafted to be processed, stamped, loaded onto a ship. Bagnoli had white, smooth concrete walls and grey, smooth concrete floors and dusty hot places between buildings where the pale sun stung your eyes and burnt your skin as you stood in the queue. At Bagnoli 169 saw what a displaced person she had become and then came the shocking truth that she had ceased to be a person altogether. She could no longer make choices; she was but one of many numbers to be drafted, processed, shipped.

A heavy numbness befell 169; she became passive, she felt ill. 'It's the food, you're not used to all that olive oil. You must eat, you mustn't let them think you're not fit to travel,' said her husband. He could not understand how she felt. He was looking forward to a new life with his new wife in a new country and he could not see that a door had closed for 169, that 'un-person' soon to be sent so far away.

Beautiful Naples. The pastel-coloured buildings, the sparkling blue waters of the bay, holidaymakers strolling along the waterfront ... 169 had only blurred glimpses of all this as she swayed, tightly wedged between the other numbers, on the tray of an open truck. Guarded by heavily armed carabinieri, she felt like a felon about to be deported. Were they guarding the refugees from the Italians and tourists or vice versa? She did not know. She could not ask. She was unloaded, then conveyed up the gangway onto the SS *Goya* berthed in the harbour.

The *Goya* was chartered by the IRO to ship refugee immigrants to Australia and New Zealand. She had a chequered history, having started her career as a banana boat plying from the German Cameroons in Africa to Germany and back and later serving as U-boat supply vessel during the Second World War. Originally designed for cargo, her huge holds had now been fitted with three-tiered bunks in blocks of six, the occasional ablution facilities, a messroom holding about 150 people, a small hospital of two cabins and a jail. Her air-conditioning and cooling system was ancient and more banana- than people-oriented. It broke down in the Suez Canal, and did not function again until the ship reached the Tasman Sea, where the weather was so cold that it was not needed any more.

The *Goya* transported 560 displaced persons to New Zealand on her second trip during July/August 1951, including Number 169 who was drafted into a dark hold – there were no portholes because it was below the waterline – to occupy the top right bunk in the middle row. There were 48 bunks in this hold: 47 were occupied by Greek- and Italian-speaking women; Bunk 48 was occupied by 169. The Mediterranean was rough and hardy sailors we were not. Although we tried to comfort each other, holding heads over buckets, mopping up, drying tears and worse, it soon became unbearable for 169 in the hold and she staggered onto the deck and over to the railings where she was sick – against the wind. This mistake, a never-to-be-forgotten moment, was a turning point. Suddenly angry, she resolved to survive, no matter what fate had in store for her.

At that moment Number 169 became a person once more. I was never seasick again. Not even when, chugging through the hot Suez Canal, the main meal of the day consisted of a piece of boiled liver, surrounded by dark purple rings of beetroot and a greyish mass of instant mashed potato. Not even in the Tasman Sea when the wind shrieked and whipped black waves so high that the flying fish flew down onto the deck.

The sea journey to New Zealand took five and a half weeks; for 18 seemingly endless days we saw only water and sky, sometimes seabirds and flying fish, and just once another ship far away on the horizon. All through the Indian Ocean my husband and I abandoned our bunks in the hold to camp and sleep on deck. We had dragged our mattresses to a sheltered place near the funnel and squatted there together with another young couple, Inge from Hamburg and Ljubo from Montenegro in Yugoslavia. Another Yugoslav, Ljubo's friend, who was lucky enough to work as assistant cook in the ship's galley, sneaked slices of fresh bread and the occasional piece of fruit to us. These offerings were a blessing, because the meals continued to be appalling, as was the sanitation. There were no recreational facilities on board, nothing to relieve boredom or tension. We sat on our mattresses and looked at the endless sea and sky until we were forced back down into the holds by inclement weather as we neared Australia.

My mother-in-law, then 60 years old, became ill and was confined to the ship's hospital, where she lay in a bunk, pale and wan and vomiting, but still stubborn enough to refuse to take the salt tablets that would have helped against dehydration. The day she knocked the glass of water containing a dissolved salt tablet from my hand I had the first premonition of the depth of her dislike of me.

From the Gulf of Aden we had traversed the Indian Ocean and rounded Australia to berth briefly at Fremantle for bunkering. We were not allowed to disembark, of course, so everybody stood at the railings, eager to gain an impression of the Antipodes. Naive visions of a tropical paradise soon faded. It was the beginning of August, and at dawn there had been a white frost glittering on deck. What we saw was not impressive. The wharf buildings looked shabby, the few wharfies who ambled about appeared rough and there was a drunk who kept waving a bottle and mouthing unintelligible things at us. One did not get the impression of a warm welcome. We were glad we did not have to stay in Australia. I remember this as the first occasion when I actually looked forward to landing in New Zealand.

CHAPTER 28

New Zealand

I t was 15 August 1951. We had arrived in the promised land. But prom- ised by whom? What actually was the promise? Doubtfully and more than a little apprehensive we watched from the railings as the *Goya* slid into the harbour. Hills, shrouded in clouds, rocks menacingly close, a few houses, very small houses, lining the narrow beachfront and clinging precariously to steep hillsides.

We were surrounded by choppy grey waves and misty rain came towards us. It was very cold, definitely not the tropical paradise my mother had so bravely and hopefully wished for us when she presented us with our pith helmets. (These were now the treasured possessions of a small Greek boy. 'It's obvious we won't need them,' Nick had muttered.) But to our great delight there had been dolphins in the channel, darting through the bow waves, guiding the ship into the harbour, and that, surely, was a good omen.

I had got up long before the crack of dawn that morning, had been the first in the communal showers, scrubbing away the miasma of the long journey, wanting to be clean to face my new home, Neuseeland, the new land across the sea. Others had similar aspirations. Memorable was the aristocratic Hun- garian princess who stood stark naked in one of the doorless shower cubicles, soaping herself vigorously. The interior gangways of the ship had been un- locked by the time she took her ablutions and men, women and children, trooping through en masse on their way to assemble their luggage on deck, were gaping at the soapy princess. My offer to hold up a concealing towel was politely declined – 'Let them look, my dear, they are just peasants, they do not matter. I wish to be clean on arrival in my chosen country.'

The ship tied up at the wharf – such a little wharf. There were railway car- riages, ready to take us to Pahiatua, the Reception and Training Centre for

Refugee Immigrants. We climbed in, each carrying our suitcases, sat on the wooden seats and looked and waited. When some stout and sensibly clad ladies came into the compartment and handed each of us a little box of biscuits, saying 'Welcome to New Zealand', we cheered up a bit. The train started to move, rattling past more little houses clinging to bush-covered hillsides. When a conductor came through our carriage I asked him, 'When do we get to Wellington, please?' He looked at me and replied, 'You've just been there, lady.' Oh. I had expected a capital city like those in Europe, with big buildings, busy streets ... I looked back through the grimy train window, but New Zealand's capital city had already disappeared into mist and rain.

We sat on the wooden railway benches, enveloped by the smell of our wet clothing, of wet, sooty grime and of the scorching heating pipes under the seats. The rivulets of water streaking the train windows made it difficult to distinguish details of the landscape. Blurred images flitted by: a rocky foreshore, with waves frothing against dark brown boulders; a series of tunnels emerging into wet, green narrow gorges, which gradually widened and led to more open country; the sturdily defiant shapes of gnarled macrocarpa trees; steep hillsides, now covered in dense glistening wet bush, now dotted with greyish white blobs – sheep grazing smooth green pastures. Some trees struggled up the flanks of the hills, their trunks and foliage leaning at a sharp angle, away from the winds of the sea. Fences snaked up the hillsides or intersected the flat ground near the railway line. And bracken, of dark green, brownish and silvery hues, encroached onto the embankments. There were no settlements resembling the villages of Germany, but isolated farmhouses, most of them sheltering within high dark hedges, with barns, sheds, fenced yards in close proximity, their link to modern technology indicated by tall wooden power poles carrying two strands of wire.

I think our train rattled through or past the townships between Wellington and Pahiatua without stopping. I can only vaguely remember little wooden houses when I try to recall Carterton and Masterton, but the name Eketahuna sticks in my memory, so intriguingly foreign and unpronounceable! We did not talk much on this train journey. Apprehensive and tired, we retreated into our own thoughts, worries and expectations. We knew so little about this land we had come to. What lay ahead of us? How would we cope with the immediate future? What was expected of us?

I recalled the meagre information I knew about New Zealand. It had some active volcanoes. The Queen of England was its sovereign. It had been discovered twice, first by Polynesians called Maori who, under the leadership of Kupe, paddled their canoe from Hawaiki to these shores, and later by a British sailing ship under Captain Cook, who brought white settlers. There had been skirmishes between the settlers and the Maori. The settlers won and took up farming. There had been a gold rush. There were no wild and dangerous animals in New Zealand, but there was a flightless nocturnal bird called kiwi. The inhabitants of New Zealand were called Kiwis, after this bird. All Kiwis liked horse racing.

I had gained this information on the *Goya*. The ship's radio had picked up a New Zealand radio station to which we listened, enthralled but bewildered. We could not understand what was said; the words all ran into each other, very fast, the voice rising to a high pitched monotone chant, with an excited crowd crescendo as background. When I enquired of the Anglican priest who was escorting us immigrants whether this radio broadcast was of a ceremony of religious fervour, he chuckled and said it had been a race commentary and that every small town in New Zealand had its own racecourse. The Maori were dark-skinned. They had been cannibals and fierce warriors. This conjured up in my mind images of noble savages, splendid warriors adorned with feathers and war paint swooping down from the hills, brandishing spears. I was determined to greet them with friendliness and as equals and to be scrupulously fair in all my dealings with them, unlike earlier white settlers. On the journey to Pahiatua I looked for Maori warriors to swoop down, but they never did, not a single one – much to my disappointment.

Pahiatua Camp: high wire fences, one wide gate and a sentry box. Was the gate locked once we were inside? Drafted into mobs according to alphabetical order of surname, we found ourselves in a large hall where wooden trestles and forms had been set up. There was a podium with the New Zealand flag and a lectern at one end of the hall, a counter with closed wooden shutters at the other. Kitchen clatter and cooking smells seeped through. An official-looking man, equipped with a clipboard and several folders, stepped up to the lectern and welcomed us to New Zealand and to Pahiatua in particular. He informed us that we were to stay at this camp until suitable jobs and accommodation had been obtained for us. We were reminded that we were under contract to work and live for the next two years wherever the government saw fit to place us and we were told that classes had been arranged to teach us 'the New Zealand way of life'.

Missing an enthusiastic response from his audience, who sat there obedient, quiet and bewildered, he deduced that he had, perhaps, been misunderstood, or not understood at all.

'Does anybody here speak English?' he boomed.

There was an embarrassed silence. When I timidly raised my hand, I was summoned to his side and found myself translating his speech into German, which most people did understand.

And then we were fed. I will never forget my first meal in New Zealand. There were stainless steel bowls containing a greenish glutinous mass in which floated indefinable greenish grey shapes and other bowls with glassy pale shreds of what I presumed to be cabbage. I could recognise the carrots and the mountains of mashed potatoes. 'Spuds', I found out, was the correct name for them and the greenish grey things were 'curried bangers'. The thin slices of white buttered bread and the tea that followed were good to eat, but the New Zealand way of life would probably take a little getting used to as far as food was concerned, I reflected.

A mistake had been made: I was classified as female, single and dependent and so was drafted into the single women's sleeping quarters. My small concrete cubicle was icy cold, with rivulets of moisture trickling down the walls. The foam mattress on the narrow cot, the stiff white cotton sheets and the two grey army blankets afforded little warmth or comfort. Wearing nearly all my clothes, I curled into a ball and shivered the night through.

Next morning things began to look up. I, 'the English-speaking lass', was drafted to office duties and Nick, probably because he appeared tall and trustworthy, was appointed block leader. This elevated position meant that he was in charge of a long barracks building which had been divided into cubicles to house about 20 family groups. One end of the barracks contained ablution facilities and the other end a room with proper walls, right up to the ceiling – the block leader's accommodation.

Our first home in New Zealand! True, it was small, but it was private. It had a door, which one could shut, a window, which one could open, a light bulb dangling from the ceiling, two camp stretchers and a small wooden school desk, complete with lift-up lid and inkwell.

The tiny proportions of our room were illustrated on the auspicious occasion of the visit of the national secretary of the New Zealand YMCA. He had come to look us over and we were trying to make a good impression. Sitting on the two camp stretchers, our knees almost touching across the room, we discussed world affairs. Suddenly Nick rose, picked up a single hair from the floor, opened the window and threw it out. Our visitor appeared startled at this action, but it made perfect sense to us. There was just not enough space in that room for three people *and* a stray hair.

CHAPTER 29

Pahiatua

We stayed in Pahiatua Camp throughout the rest of August and September. Nick was busy leading his block, which involved keeping law and order and seeing to it that people did their rostered duties. His parents, who were finding it hard to adjust to the new environment they found themselves in, were spending most of their time earnestly trying to learn English and coming to terms with the unfamiliar customs of this land, so far removed from their beloved Russia. Their leisure time was spent in the company of compatriots, bemoaning their fate, complaining about their present situation and worrying about their future.

And I was gainfully employed, for £10 a week, after deduction of tax and board. In the camp office my job was to carefully, neatly and confidentially copy people's personal particulars from grey cards onto brownish yellow cards, then file them into cardboard boxes in alphabetical order and find them again when required. The finding again was the hard bit; I have never been a very methodical person. When I ran out of people, particulars and cardboard boxes, I was promoted to telephone operator. The telephone switchboard was made up of two boards. The upright board had 86 extensions, little metal doors, numbered, which flipped down with an apologetic-sounding click, exposing small plug holes. The desk board was more assertive. It had 15 plug holes, displaying red lights for incoming calls and angry sounding buzzers. There was a tangle of cords, with plugs at each end, and a headset with a microphone. The trick was to connect the right plug with the right hole, not to get fazed by angry buzzers and to warble the correct formula into the microphone without tripping over your tongue: 'This is the office of the Pahiatua Reception and Training Centre, can I help you?' The fun bit was to listen in for a moment and then say, ' Working? Working?' Sometimes I pulled the plug on them and cut them off. And when they buzzed again, I said, 'Sorry, you were discon-nected.' True, except for the 'sorry'.

Once or twice, on a Friday night, Nick and I went into Pahiatua itself. This involved getting a taxi – frivolous expense! – and then strolling along the main street of the town, looking into shop windows. We went up the left side of the street and back down the right side. It did not take long: Pahiatua is not very big, or exciting.

The houses along the main street were mostly one-storeyed buildings, many sporting false facades to make them look more imposing. All along the shopfronts ran corrugated iron-covered verandahs, sloped, or sometimes curved elegantly, which were supported by slender wooden or iron posts. These cre-ated an atmosphere reminiscent of the Wild West towns in cowboy movies.

Milkbars were a new experience for us. A few formica-covered tables with plastic floral arrangements adorned one side of the shop, a long counter in front of high shelves the other. Displayed on these were tins of biscuits and cardboard boxes containing such delights as liquorice strips, cinnamon bars and chocolate fish. A glass-fronted cabinet on the counter contained triangles of sandwiches and various 'fancy cakes'. A heated cabinet next to it kept mince pies, bacon and egg pies and sausage rolls at a temperature that guaranteed they were dry and mummified when purchased. Also on the counter were large glass jars out of which one could buy formidable gob-stoppers, multi-hued all-day suckers, black and white striped peppermints and wine gums in the shape of aeroplanes or snakes. Threepence or sixpence worth of these were carefully counted into a small paper bag. One could buy milkshakes of vari-ous sweet flavours and hues, whizzed frothy in a noisy contraption and served in fluted metal beakers, with a straw by request. Our biggest thrill always was to buy an ice cream. For 1 shilling and sixpence you got a triple-decker: three scoops of delicious ice cream balanced precariously on top of a crisp cone. Our favourite was hokey pokey, that rich creamy vanilla ice cream hiding crunchy caramelised sugar lumps. This was a Kiwi icon, at that time unknown to the rest of the world.

We also went to the picture theatre, with a downstairs and an upstairs. Down-stairs was cheap and noisy, upstairs more refined and costly; we went upstairs. The seats, covered with dark brown oilcloth, squeaked when you tipped them to sit down and again as they sprang back up. Reddish velvet curtains slid aside to reveal the screen on which the white numbers 4-3-2-1 appeared within a black circle. The film was about to begin, but no – a roll of drums and every-

Our wedding on 11 June 1950. The civil ceremony was followed later by a service in the Russian Orthodox Church.

With Nick at Kreuth. My sister called us 'the turtle doves'.

Arrival in New Zealand – new immigrants clutching their belongings as they wait for the train that would take them to the Refugee Immigrant Reception Centre.

Pahiatua, our first 'home' in New Zealand.

LEFT: Nikolaj Jaklevich and Jekaterina Wassilevna – Nick's parents – came to New Zealand on the *Goya* with us.

Nick working on the Roxburgh dam site.

Roxburgh in the 1950s: raw new
terraces of look-alike houses.

The swing-bridge I crossed every day
on my way to work at the jam factory.

Social life in Roxburgh in the 1950s: men got together with their 'mates' and women's lives revolved around their homes and children.

The kitchen of our first real home in New Zealand.

Michael, our own little Kiwi.

body stood up, with a squeak and clatter of seats, and began to sing 'God Save Our Gracious King'. People looked at us, so we stood up too. When the singing had finished, we all squeaked our seats down again and watched the news-reels: in black and white we could see what the faraway world was up to. And then the feature film started. Halfway through, probably when the projection-ist had to change reels, there was the interval. The lights came on, some people squeaked out of their seats to go outside and a man in white overalls appeared in the aisle. He had a large tray suspended from shoulder straps from which he sold vanilla ice cream in cones. A wonderful custom! We avidly adopted it but sadly it did not survive the modernisation of cinemas; somewhere along the path of emancipation it fell by the wayside, along with the obligatory singing of the British National Anthem.

After two months at Pahiatua Camp, having been trained in the ways of the world down under, we felt ready to try out our newly acquired skills and so we travelled to Wellington for a weekend. I can still hear the clickety clack, clickety clack clack, click, as the railcar rattled along. I was fascinated by the ingenious method of mailbags being snatched up by a hook from poles spaced along the line.

Wellington in 1951 was not the vibrant, colourful city it is today. The smart high-rise buildings, glitzy shops, upmarket restaurants and tiled pavements that give the inner city its present cosmopolitan look were still only a gleam in town planners' eyes. The inner city we saw was of small town appearance, solid, staid, in need of a coat of paint. Corrugated iron verandahs, much like the ones in Pahiatua, cracked pavements, wooden power poles and lots of wires criss-crossing overhead. There were numerous small shops, most of them dark and locked – no weekend shopping in those days! The houses were big-ger than those in Pahiatua; there were red brick walls and some narrow alleys between buildings, where rubbish piled up in drums. The few pedestrians we encountered were very ordinary-looking too.

We stayed at the People's Palace, which was run by the Salvation Army and was recommended as clean, safe and reasonably priced. It was all of these, and frugal, with two chaste single beds in our room, Bibles on the bedside tables and a solitary light bulb dangling from the ceiling, its switch far away from the beds. The facilities were at the end of a long, linoleum-covered corridor. The enamel bath had most of its enamel scoured away and the shower, attached over the plug end, emitted only a tired trickle of lukewarm water. They served rubbery eggs for breakfast but were generous with toast and marmalade and offered kind advice. The museum and the Houses of Parliament were deemed suitable for sightseeing but 'stay away from Cuba Street' they warned, without elaborating.

Of course we went; we had come to experience all the capital city could offer and the implied naughtiness of Cuba Street drew us like a magnet. But it all seemed so boring, grey and dingy and ordinary. It was a bit run down and seedy, certainly, but it did not give the impression of being a place of great depravity. We could not fathom why we had been advised not to go there – no vice to be seen. We wandered into a Chinese fish and chip restaurant. The front shop seemed respectable, but when we were ushered into the dining room, with its darkish green walls, red formica tables and one or two lanterns casting more shadows than light, we felt distinctly uneasy. 'Let's sit with our backs against the wall,' whispered Nick. We were the only diners. Other customers, all Asian, flitted through the room and disappeared through a swing door at the far end. Every time this door opened there issued a muted babble of voices and an indefinable acrid smell. The fish and chips were tasty but we did not do them justice. We were glad to escape out onto the street again, without knives sticking in our backs. An opium den? A gambling place? Whatever it was, it emanated sinister vibes!

And so we walked on through Cuba Street, hand in hand. Suddenly there were glad cries from an upstairs window: 'Nick, Helga, good to see you, come up, come on up, quickly!' Sarah, Isaak and their son, little Ralph, had been our travelling companions on the *Goya*. They had left Pahiatua Camp almost immediately because the Jewish Committee had provided the walk-up flat in Cuba Street and a job for Isaak. Sarah still had a number tattooed on her forearm, marking her as former inmate of a concentration camp. Ralph had been called Wolfgang when we embarked but once over the equator he became Ralph, a change of name to which he adapted without fuss. They were practical people, these three, survivors who were determined to make the best of any circumstances they found themselves in.

Isaak had boarded the *Goya* carrying a large bag of garlic to keep scurvy at bay during the long ocean voyage. He and Nick had been allocated adjoining narrow bunks. Separated only by a metal bar, they spent the first uncomfortable nights in furtive combat, digging knees or elbows into each other, one snoring intermittently, the other one breathing out garlic fumes. But, practical man that he was, Isaak had soon found an amiable solution: they would both turn in unison, gently nudging each other to the right or to the left as required, sharing both the garlic and the snoring. This close physical proximity, the orchestrated nightly ballet movements and the haze of garlic fumes enveloping the pair formed the basis of our friendship.

Glad to see each other again, we had much to talk and laugh about. Isaak trotted out a big colourful and lumpy eiderdown. 'Feel this,' he chuckled. 'What do you think is in it? I've got 25 gold watches sewn inside!' Sarah, not to be outdone, beckoned us into the bedroom. Under the bed was a flagon containing 2 litres of Chanel No. 5. To prove it was the real thing she squirted liberal amounts all over us, so that we reeked of the strong perfume. Even the next day, when we were walking along the street, people turned and stared at us, as we wafted past. We had a lovely Kaffeeklatsch, with a lace tablecloth, Rosenthal china, silver cutlery, the lot.

Suddenly there was a knock and shout at the downstairs door: the Jewish Committee was paying a visit. Sarah and Isaak swang into action. China, silver, tablecloth were whipped away, bundled into the oven with lightning speed. By the time the Jewish Committee had mounted the stairs, we were sitting demurely around a bare wooden table, poor refugees, grateful for charity. Sarah just winked slightly at me as we took our leave.

CHAPTER 30

Roxburgh

We were delighted when we were told that employment had been found for Nick. He was to work as chain man for the Survey Department of the Ministry of Works at the Roxburgh hydro project in Central Otago, where a dam was taking shape across the mighty Clutha River to provide power for the national grid. In the 1950s this was New Zealand's most ambitious undertaking. Apart from the Ministry of Works, British and Swiss firms had been contracted to manage the project and the workforce comprised men of many nationalities. To accommodate the thousands of workers, a camp for single men had been set up on the hill adjacent to the dam face on the west side of the Clutha.

The men lived in single huts and shared ablution facilities, with communal meals provided by a cookhouse. On the higher river terraces were the project's administration buildings, the shopping centre, a large community hall and the staff houses for management officials and their families. These houses, painted, were larger and had fenced gardens. On the lower terraces were the many smaller look-alike houses occupied by married workers. They were set out along sweeping curved roads with names like Bendigo Crescent and Kohinoor Street. Shingled river flats, criss-crossed by supply roads, lay between the hydro village and the Clutha. Huge Euclid trucks, carrying big boulders, cranes and other heavy machinery, hissed and rumbled along these roads, shaking the earth as they lumbered past. Like prehistoric monsters, they gouged and bit and scraped into the rock, reshaping the ancient valley, altering the course of old man Clutha.

The hills rose, solid and silent, on both sides of the valley floor, unaffected by all the change wrought at their feet. Dark, rocky and barren, they towered to the south-west of the valley, sparsely covered by snowgrass, tussock and spiky matagouri. A few hardy merino sheep grazed there, but these hills belonged to the rabbits, millions of which lived, bred and burrowed all over the steep slopes. Coming over the crest of a ridge we once beheld a startling sight: the whole hillside seemed to move, as thousands of small furry animals scampered to the safety of their burrows. Bad weather came from that side of the hills, with grey shrouds clawing their way over the tops to envelop the valley with cold misty rain or menacing clouds building up and up into the darkening sky beyond before crashing their load of hard rain or sleet into the valley. The hills to the east were also topped by rocky crags, called The Nobbies, with the Two Thumbs the highest outcrop towards the south. But these hills were of a much gentler slope and disposition. Lying to the sun, orchards blossomed on their flanks, spilling across the river terraces right down to the edge of the Clutha. The famous Roxburgh apricots ripened there, along with peaches, nectarines, plums, apples, raspberries and boysenberries.

Our first real home in New Zealand was the little house we were allocated in the village, at 152 Kohinoor Street. The standard Ministry of Works design for married workers at hydro schemes, it was built in a T shape, with two small bedrooms, one at each side of the open-plan kitchen-dining-living room, with its black Shacklock coal range for cooking and heating. The entrance was through an open porch at the rear of the house, the door to the left leading into kitchen, the door straight ahead to 'out the back', which was the bathroom-cum-laundry with a concrete tub, a copper, a tin bath and, behind a partition, the toilet. The house, which sat on cylindrical concrete piles, was made of wood, creosoted dark brown, with a touch of white around the windows, and the roof was covered with black malthoid tarred paper. Inside, there were bare floorboards and 'stable doors' and the walls seemed to be of cardboard – gib board, it was called.

The patch of ground surrounding the house was stony, with a sparse covering of weeds and a few clumps of yellow river lupins. A steep shingle bank at the back of 'the section' rose up to the road along which thundered the huge articulated trucks, carrying rocks and boulders to and from the dam site. The houses on both sides of ours and as far as the eye could see were of identical design, but some of them were already loved and lived in, with letterboxes, flower beds and a bit of lawn round the front, clotheslines, wood bins and a 'vege garden' round the back.

We unlocked our door. The key proved to be identical to all the other house keys along the street. This was 'handy' as it gave you easy access to your neighbour's premises, if you were asked to water the pot plants or feed the cat while they were away on holiday. The only time you might lock your place was if you went away for a few days. The key was then usually hidden in a safe place, under the door mat or on a nail in the wood box. As far as I know, nothing was ever stolen in the village during those innocent days.

Inside, in the middle of the bare floor, stood the two boxes containing all our worldly goods and five big tins of cream paint with a large paintbrush. We looked at each other silently: Our pioneering days had begun, and so had our pioneering nights. The first night in our new home we spent sleeping in our clothes on the bare floor, wrapped in everything we could lay our hands on, and we were still cold. Sometime in the early hours of the morning there was a loud crash at the door. A kindly soul, we never found out who he was, had left a sack of wood blocks and kindling in the porch and we managed to light a fire in the coal range. After successfully experimenting with the flue handle and the damper and getting rid of the choking smoke that had filled the room, we became quite cosy and warm and things began to look up.

We met our neighbours. The people next door, Joy and Sid, became our good friends and mentors. Sid was a truck driver who thundered around in one of those huge articulated beasts during working hours and drove a taxi in his spare time. It was he who solved our interior decorating problem: 'Just get a few flagons of beer, plenty of saveloys, tomato sauce, bread and butter and me and the boys will give you a hand with the painting.'

Sid was as good as his word. Next morning he and the boys turned up. Capable men, equipped with brushes, paint rollers and a transistor radio, they slapped paint on ceiling and walls with great skill and speed, good-naturedly instructing Nick how to wield a brush and me how to cook saveloys in the copper after the first batch had messily split their skins. The beer flowed, the paint flowed, the music got louder and louder, the jokes got funnier and funnier, reaching heights beyond our understanding. By and by the saveloys were heated to perfection too. Everybody had a rip-roaring good time and everything in our house that stood still for long enough, with the exception of the coal range, was painted cream that day. We were delighted, grateful and confused. The fair dinkum Kiwi spirit of helpfulness and know-how had passed over us like a steamroller. Our first experience of it was wonderful, but I have not been partial to saveloys since.

We laid congoleum on the floor. This was thick cardboard, with tar paint on the underside and lacquered with shiny patterns on top. Cheaper than linoleum, easy to keep clean, congoleum was the fashionable floor covering of most houses in the hydro village. The furniture arrived, I sewed curtains for the bare windows, we planted poplars and started a vege patch 'round the back', put in a few flowers and rolled a pocket handkerchief-sized piece of stony ground for a future front lawn – all under Sid's guidance.

Joy became my special adviser on domestic matters and later my business partner. Our friendship started the day she came to the fence and yoo-hooed me over: 'Excuse me,' she said, 'but if you carry on like this, you'll have no sheets left.' I was washing the bed linen. Having dragged our kitchen table outside, I had spread a sheet on top and was belabouring it with a strong scrubbing brush dipped in Sunlight soapy water. I thought this was the correct way, having vague recollections of seeing the Greek or Italian women at Bagnoli camp scrubbing their washing and beating it upon stones. I would have done the beating too but for the lack of suitably big boulders.

Joy showed me the right way. You filled the copper with cold water, lit a fire underneath and then used a cheese grater to flake a cake of Sunlight soap into the water. When it was all bubbly and hot you put your linen into the copper, stirring it every now and then with a huge wooden spoon. The hard part was to fish it out, still hot, and plunge it into cold water in the tub. It had to be rinsed twice, Joy instructed me, before it could be wrung out and put on the clothes-line. The line was a long piece of No.8 wire, threaded through the top of two poles, which Sid had acquired for us by courtesy of the carpenters' depot. The washing was hoisted into the wind with the aid of long manuka stakes, forked at the top. Washing 'the smalls' was much easier as they required no boiling. They were soaped and rubbed up and down a corrugated washboard, before being rinsed twice.

Doing the washing became my first commercial enterprise in New Zealand. One day Joy and I hit on the brilliant idea of running a laundry service for the 700 or so single men who worked at the hydro. We drew a cardboard poster advertising our services and nailed it to the door of the single men's kitchen. The venture was a great success right from the word go. Single men, all making good money, did not want to be bothered with washing their shirts and socks, so we did it for them, and charged outrageous rates: 2 shillings for socks, 1 shilling for a hankie, 7 shillings and sixpence for a shirt and so on.

We were very well organised. On Monday morning the taxi man collected 'the dirties' and delivered them to us in bundles. We then sat on the doorstep and marked the stuff. This was a fairly unpleasant and smelly job, but it had to be done to ensure our customers got the correct set of clothes back. All Monday and most of Tuesday we washed. As we had invested in two Pallo washing machines, the latest models with automatic wringers on top, this was not too bad, and we churned out batch after batch of washing, letting it flutter in the breeze in our back yards, now criss-crossed by several clotheslines. On Wednesday and Thursday we ironed. One summer's day it was 105 degrees Fahrenheit and I had to iron 79 shirts. Friday was the most enjoyable day of our working week. The washing was folded and put into nice and tidy brown paper parcels which we tied with string, twisting the account, for cash of course, into the knot on top. The taxi man delivered the parcels and collected our money. Our customers were always pleased to pay on delivery and he brought the cash to us. We deducted our expenses, the fee for the taxi man, the hire purchase instalment for the washing machines and the soap and deposited the rest, a pleasing pile of notes and coins, in a biscuit tin. Whenever it was overflowing, we toddled off to the Post Office Savings Bank.

Everything went well, apart from an occasional hiccup. Once a whole machine load of white dress shirts turned pink, probably the result of a wicked ballpoint pen sneaking into the Pallo. After a few desperate experiments, I found the cure: each individual shirt was pressure-cooked in Janola bleach. That fixed them; they were snowy white again, although the fabric looked a bit fragile after the treatment. As our enterprise flourished we added refinements, such as sending the white collars of dress shirts, which had to be starched, to a Chinese laundry in Dunedin. It was fun to occasionally recognise our customers by the clothes they wore, but we always kept to decorous anonymity, resisting the impulse to greet Mr Blue Checked Shirt or Mr Red, Green and Black Patterned Socks.

It never occurred to Joy or me that we should have had a permit, let alone pay income tax for our business. We were surprised and shocked when a nasty little official turned up one day, pointing out the error of our ways and the possible dire consequences thereof. Sadly we terminated our laundry services. Joy decided to have her second child and started knitting booties and I found another job, at the Roxdale jam factory, on the other side of the Clutha.

A swing-bridge with wooden planks and wire mesh sides was strung high above the swirling blue waters and this I crossed to get to work, not daring to look down, eyes fixed on the other bank and both hands firmly on the wires on each side. I worked in the office; actually I was the office. The manager was far too busy organising the fruit to come in, supervising the cooking and canning process and dispatching the product all over the country, to bother about the clerical side. I was installed on a high three-legged stool in front of a slanting desk and told to 'just get on with it' and 'you'll soon get the hang of it'.

I had two friends to help me: the cash register and the Ready Reckoner. The impressive cash register had silvery metal decorations all over its cast iron body and a lever to pull at its side. A bell pinged when you operated the lever and a drawer flew open, revealing neat little compartments filled with notes and coins. We had ha'pennies, pennies, florins and half-crowns and, of course, pounds and shillings, sixpences and threepences then. When he returned from the bank, the manager carried the pound notes in grey linen bags and the coins in stout brown paper bags and I then sorted the money into its compartments in the drawer. It had to come out again to be inserted into small brown envelopes, as wages for the employees. I wrote the name on each envelope, the hours worked and the hourly rate, the overtime and rate, the gross amount, the deductions and finally the net amount.

All this was calculated from the time sheets which were filled out by each employee every day and spiked on a long nail at the exit door of the factory. I picked these up first thing in the morning and entered the particulars in 'the book' from which the weekly wage was calculated. This was where the Ready Reckoner proved invaluable.

It was also a friend in need when it came to working out payment for the growers. The fruit came in an assortment of weird weights and measures. Raspberries, loganberries and blackcurrants came in kerosene tins, strawberries in pottles or on trays, apricots, peaches, nectarines and plums came either in bushels or hundredweights, which were not 100 but 110 pounds and a pound was not 500 but 450 grams and a bushel was 56 pounds of 450 grams each.

The raspberries, loganberries and strawberries came from as far as Waimate, the apricots, nectarines, peaches and plums were grown in Roxburgh, Dunbarton, Ettrick, Millers Flat and upstream as far as Alexandra and Cromwell, and in all the orchards on both sides of the Clutha valley. Several of the local fruit growers became our friends. One let me ride her big brown hunter, and others invited us for afternoon teas, always formal affairs when stockings were worn, even if it was 106 degrees Fahrenheit in the shade. The factory staff was made up of 'seasonals', who stayed in the bunkhouse, usually for a short time only. They worked shifts and overtime, sorting and stoning fruit from hoppers on long belts. The cooking and canning was done by the 'permanents', reliable long-term employees who knew just the right moment when the fruit and sugar in the huge vats had bubbled to the perfection required for canning. We all had our tea breaks, on the dot of ten and three, at a bare wooden table in the 'smoko' room, decorated with posters of Roxdale products and the fire drill regulations. The tea lady served tea and scones. It was an enjoyable experience to work at the jam factory and I left only when it became difficult for me to tiptoe across the swing-bridge and to fit my big pregnant tummy between the stool and the slanting desk. They gave me presents of booties and bonnets at the farewell morning tea, for which I had 'shouted' cream cakes, as was the custom.

Nick was climbing the ladder of professional success. He had been sent to work at the dam as assistant chain man, attached to the Survey Department. After six months he was promoted to chain man, which meant he was allowed to carry a wooden pole with markings, a reel of tape and a clipboard. Occasionally he was permitted to peer through the theodolite to take readings in unfamiliar measurements of distance, such as inches, feet, chains and miles. True, he still went to work at seven, equipped with his lunch-tin and flask, and came home after five, dusty and tired, but his wages had gone up and he rode to work on a second-hand bone-shaker bike.

We both had an evening job. The benevolent godfathers of the YMCA, knowing that we needed to make money, had offered Nick the job of doorman at the picture theatre they ran in the community hall. His task was to unlock the premises before the shows, secure them afterwards and keep the audience in order in between. As sign of office, he carried a torch with a powerful beam. He performed his duties most efficiently and with a minimum of fuss. Walking up and down on either side of the auditorium in the flickering darkness, he only had to direct the torch beam towards any potential troublemaker for him to 'pull his head in' and settle down. The reason for this instant obedience? Somebody had spread the rumour the Nick had been a martial arts champion in the Red Army. We never dispelled this belief.

My job was less glamorous. I was one of the team of three women, 'girls' we were called then, who made up the front of house team. We took turns selling tickets, ripping them in half at the entrance and ushering late-comers to empty seats, or selling sweets. The latter was the most popular task, as we were allowed to keep, that meant eat, any chocolate bar or lolly from a damaged packet. 'Oops,' we'd say, 'what a shame, it's damaged!' and share the contents of the damaged packet. My sweet tooth probably dates back to that time.

CHAPTER 31

The Learning Years

Those first five years at Roxburgh were learning years. We learned to adapt to the ways of our new homeland, fit in with the social environment. We coped with the day-to-day challenges of work and housekeeping and got used to the climate and the reversal of seasons: Christmas in summer at 103 degrees Fahrenheit, balloons on the Christmas tree, roast lamb, mint sauce and pavlova instead of the traditional goose, dumplings and marzipan. It was hard to fight homesickness.

The workforce at the hydro was multi-national. Professionals working for the Ministry of Works, together with the staff of the British and Swiss contractors, formed the top of the hierarchy. The workers came from all over New Zealand and there were many immigrants from England and Holland, a sprinkling of Poles, Greeks, Yugoslavs, Czechs and us two: one Russian, one German.

Owing to recent historic events and the propaganda that followed, Russians and particularly Germans were perceived as 'baddies' in the 1960s. To some extent even now, more than 50 years and two generations after the atrocities of the Second World War, this perception is still perpetuated by some of the media. It is to the credit of the many people we met in those early days that they saw past this barrier and became our good friends. The friendships established at Roxburgh have lasted and grown to this day.

Nick had more language difficulties than I, but both our vocabularies increased rapidly, especially in the area of Kiwi slang, which our co-workers and neighbours delighted in teaching us. Many words and phrases, tripping so lightly from my tongue, made me blush when their meaning was translated to me, much later, by the conservative and staid good folk of Stratford in Taranaki.

Nick's initiation ceremony to qualify as 'one of the blokes' was a garage party, thrown by Sid, our good neighbour. 'No women allowed, but bring a dozen,' Sid had instructed. So off Nick went, only to reappear a few minutes later. 'Quick, give me lots of dry bread and some olive oil, there's going to be some serious drinking!' Thus fortified he sallied forth again, not to return until the early hours, pale but triumphant. 'Sid and I were the only ones still on our feet at two o'clock,' he announced, 'and Sid slid under the trestle table soon after.' None of the blokes had known of the Russian trick for coping with large quantities of booze: dry bread to soak it up and olive oil to float on top. At work the next day Nick was winked at, slapped on the back and hailed as a mate. He had gained recognition and respect. Now he was one of them.

Later he had more Kiwi experience of alcohol. 'Trevor knew all about it,' they said. He had been making home brew for years, Trevor had, good beer too – carried quite a kick. It put hair on your chest, Trevor's brew, and it was much cheaper than the bought stuff. Nothing to it, just follow Trevor's instructions. Easy. Trevor had all the gear and they'd get the whole job done on a Saturday morning. It would save a lot of money: they would share the cost of the ingredients, which did not come to much.

All they had to bring was 5 dozen empties each. 'Rinse 'em out a bit' had been the only advice given. And so it came to pass that two apprentice brewers and one expert sat on the doorstep of the wash-house one fine Saturday morning: Jos the Dutchman, Trevor from the survey office and my Nick. They talked a lot of men talk and laughed belly laughs and followed Trevor's easy instructions. He had filled the copper, stoked it up to bubbling point and they had all taken turns adding secret ingredients under his guidance, stirring them around with a broom handle. The mixture smelt of yeast and malt and sugar, quite nice really, but not much like beer. It lacked something, a bit of oomph.

'Ah,' said Trevor. 'I know. Needs a bit of thyme, it does. Thyme gives it a lift.' Jos sped away on his bike and returned with a bunch of wild thyme from the roadside and they chucked it into the bubbling brew. A strong herbal odour resulted. 'She'll be right now,' said Trevor, 'ready for bottling.'

He had all the necessary gear – pouring jugs, funnels, proper metal bottle tops and a gadget for pressing them on firmly – and by late afternoon they had filled and capped 108 bottles. The three gentlemen, very happy and pleased with their achievement, surveyed the result of their labours. The bottles did looked neat, all sitting there in rows. 'You'll have to lay them on their side and let them mature now,' said Trevor. 'I reckon six weeks will do it. Cool place. Under the house is best.' Jos was the thinnest so he squirmed past the concrete piles and found the coolest place, under our bedroom. Nick passed the bottles to Jos, who tenderly laid them side by side on the gravelly sand. Trevor cleaned out the copper and then rested on his laurels, enjoying a smoke and the admiration of his pals.

Six weeks passed, the day of the beer tasting had come. Friends had been invited, Jos crawled under the house again and the first six bottles were triumphantly unearthed, wiped, admired and uncapped. The brew frothed over, confirming that it had fermented properly and was the strong, good stuff Trevor had predicted. 'Down the hatch,' they cried and 'Here's to us!' as they swigged a hearty mouthful. And their faces fell. 'God,' said one. 'Shit,' said another. Nobody looked at Trevor when he mumbled, 'Musta been the bloody thyme.' One hundred and two bottles were left entombed under our house.

During the following months we were frequently woken at night by a loud boom, but the muffled explosions did not worry us unduly: we knew by the putrid odour of fermenting thyme filtering through the floorboards of our bedroom that yet another bottle had blown to smithereens.

The social scene for married women at the hydro – there were no resident single women as far as I could see – revolved around afternoon teas, either at one another's houses or at Women's Division meetings, which were held once a month in the community hall. You dressed up. For Women's Division you wore hat and gloves, even in the heat of summer, and you were expected to 'bring a plate'. That there was something edible on the plate which would not disgrace you in the eyes of all other veteran cake-baking matrons, became a challenge. There was usually a lady speaker – 'My visit to …' – or a demonstration of cake icing, the art of making crepe paper flowers and suchlike. This entertainment was preceded by minutes of the previous meeting, matters arising and remits to conference, all serious stuff to which we said 'Aye'. Nobody ever rose to the contrary bait. The meetings always opened with 'God Save the Queen' and closed with the formal Women's Division prayer. You went home exhausted and uplifted.

Afternoon tea at a friend's house was less formal, but a certain etiquette still had to be observed. As hostess you provided something buttered, something plain, something iced, something creamed and something savoury, and tea; we did not drink coffee then. As a guest you were expected to arrive not before half past two, but no later than quarter to three and to take your leave promptly, when the whistle blew, at five o'clock.

Dinner parties were not in vogue then; an evening invitation was for supper. This was served no later than nine thirty and included hot savouries. At suppers there was mixed company, men and women, but the two sexes did not really mix. The men congregated on one side of the room, the women on the other. Our conversation was about babies, women's ailments, domestic incidents. They talked about? Only once did I cross the floor to find out, perhaps to join in the conversation. The women looked daggers, the men were embarrassed. A major faux pas by me, not to be repeated.

The houses in the hydro village were all of the same design, although larger families had single men's huts tacked on at one end or the other. This was convenient, as you knew exactly where all facilities were when you went visiting. The decor was much the same too. Congoleum or lino on the floor was usual throughout the house. Those who had been there for a while, and could afford luxuries, had carpets in the living and dining areas. These were patterned, usually in autumn tones. Curtains and bedspreads were chenille and candlewick, either maroon, beige, rose or green. Net curtains had intricate floral designs and ruffles. Settees and chairs were covered in uncut moquette and most of the furniture was stained dark brown. The entrance door was kept open in warm weather by a doorstop; the most popular design was a plaster spaniel with black and white patches. Wintry draughts under doors were kept at bay by a long sausage-shaped contraption, cutely fashioned to look like a dog or cat. To keep the flies out, one had multi-coloured plastic strips dangling in the doorway, and to deal with the flies that got in, sticky fly-paper strips dangling from light fittings, festooned with corpses.

The sign of good housekeeping was to have your Shacklock range black-leaded so that you could see your face reflected in it. To achieve this you applied graphite with a brush. Usually I ended up with my face and hands as black as the Shacklock. The concrete hearth was painted red or green and waxed, of course. Nylon fabrics in pastel colours, crimplene, glazed cotton, boldly rose-patterned, stiffened petticoats, beehive hairdos were the epitome of fashion. A-line dresses and flares for the gents came a little later. You wore an apron when doing housework or cooking; efficient and frugal housewives made these out of bleached flour bags.

Milk was milk then: there was no low fat or homogenised. The milkman ladled your pints into the billy can and the butcher sold meat from the open back of his van. Meat, milk and other perishables were kept in the safe, a box with wire mesh on three sides, attached to the outside of your kitchen wall, with the door opening above the sink. The shopping list was less complicated than it is today. At the grocer you had the choice of white bread or brown bread, mild or tasty cheese, long- or short-grain rice, white or wholemeal flour. Apart from macaroni, pasta was as yet foreign and unobtainable. A sausage was either a banger or a saveloy, both seemingly sold by the yard, or luncheon sausage of rubbery consistency in hues of pink and grey. The greengrocer supplied the vegetables you did not manage to grow in your own vege patch and, most important, the boxes of fruit you carted home by the stack to process into preserves and jam.

Spaghetti bolognese and meatballs, stuffed peppers and tomatoes with creamed potato and a few salads were about the extent of my culinary repertoire when I was first married and I had to learn fast at Roxburgh. The only alternative to cooking was to get fish 'n' chips. 'You must enjoy having all that wonderful food here in New Zealand,' I was told on numerous occasions. I always smiled a polite affirmative, but wondered secretly what people's perception of European cuisine was.

One day I needed to purchase a bra. This was not, as it turned out, a simple and straightforward affair, because I did not know the word for this garment. My colloquial English was not up to scratch and my little pocket dictionary was of no help at all. There was no 'bra' to be found; decorum forbade it, perhaps because brassiere was a French word and therefore considered risqué.

The township of Roxburgh was graced by one draper's shop, Laloli Bros, an old and venerable establishment with brass letters embellishing the windows, a polished mahogany counter and dark shelving inside. There were lots of drawers, all closed, two glass-fronted cabinets containing hats and gloves, some bolts of material, but not one bra.

Mr Laloli, an elderly gentleman, standing rotund and bald-headed behind his counter, had watched me with increasing concern as I searched. 'Can I help you?' he finally murmured, peering at me over the top of his half-round spectacles. And I, frustrated by not seeing the article I wanted, and worse, not knowing the English word for it, went up to him, looked him straight in the eye and said in a firm voice, 'I want a bosom holder!' That this was merely the literal translation of the German word for a bra, Büstenhalter, and not a brazen proposal from a foreign young woman, poor Mr Laloli did not know. The effect of my request was startling. He blushed, removed his spectacles, gripped the counter with both hands for a moment and then fled. In three strides he had reached the safety of a velvet curtain and vanished behind it.

A muffled conversation ensued, after which his head cautiously reappeared through a fold of the curtain. 'My wife will be with you in a moment,' he quavered. She, sensible matron that she was, had me sorted out in a minute – 'It's a bra you want, dearie' – and it was a simple transaction from then on. But Mr Laloli never came out again and when I visited his shop some weeks later, he retreated behind the curtain as I entered. His wife served me.

A proud new father taking his baby for a walk. Our European friends would have been astonished to see this photograph!

Nick and Michael.

Michael and friend. As a little boy he was enamoured of frogs.

Katerina with Indi and Sonja with Sharif, a photo taken after a long trek they made through the Hakataramea Valley.

We realised our dream of moving on to the land – our own piece of paradise. Riding Sharif (left), and with my beloved goats.

Our family at the wedding of Katerina and Mark, 10 December 1994. From left: Richard, Sonja, Nick, Katerina, Mark, Helga, Amanda, Michael.

The new generation: Tatjana at 16 months.

With Nick and the two most important 'people' at our place: giant Schnauzers Max (left) and Phoebe.

Thirty-year-old Indi lives in peaceful retirement on our smallholding– as do we!

CHAPTER 32

Michael

We wanted to have a family, hoped for a child in a vague sort of way, but nothing had happened during four years of marriage. I knew very little about the business of having a baby. My mother had been obtuse on this subject and there were no ante-natal classes at the hydro. When I occasionally began to feel queasy, it did not occur to me to check my dates; I was four months 'gone' when the pregnancy was confirmed by our doctor.

It was about this time that I started having cravings, particularly for German liver pâté, unobtainable in New Zealand. My mother, delighted at the news that she was to become a grandmother, at once dispatched two cans, but the New Zealand Customs Department informed us that the parcel had been confiscated by their office in Dunedin. Because the import of meat products was not allowed, my liver pâté would have to be destroyed. I rang up, explained my position and asked if I could come and eat the pâté at their office. Yes I could, so, equipped with a can opener and two packets of water biscuits, I went by bus to Dunedin. The customs officers probably thought that I was a trifle strange, but after I had persuaded them to taste a liver pâté cracker or two, we had a ball and ate the lot. I have to admit that I felt slightly nauseous after the first can, but I persevered and it cured my craving for the stuff. Not for many years could I even think about liver pâté.

Under the guidance of my good neighbour Joy and other knowledgeable friends I knitted matinée jackets, booties and helmets, bonnets and singlets, sewed gowns and petticoats, sheets and pillowcases, crocheted around pilchers and dry cot blankets. We invested in a pram, a cane bassinet and a cot. When I had expanded to alarming proportions, Nick looked upon me like a time bomb, anxiously enquiring whether 'its' arrival was imminent every time I felt a twinge.

The evening the twinges finally became serious, he panicked, vaulting over the fence to our good neighbours to get Sid and his car. They installed me on the back seat and we sped to the maternity hospital at Roxburgh. Upon arrival, he and Sid leapt out of the car and ran up to the entrance, shouting 'Sister, sister!', leaving me stranded like a beached whale. The matron appeared and asked, 'Which of you two gentlemen is having the baby?' whereupon they shamefacedly turned back to extract me and my suitcase.

I was 'prepped', put to bed, the waters broke, our doctor came and then nothing much happened. Sid took Nick home. Events took a dramatic turn later on that night and it became obvious that specialist help was required. The ambulance and Nick were sent for and at two o'clock in the morning we set off to Queen Mary Hospital in Dunedin, then a three-hour journey on metalled roads. I remember little of this as my doctor administered gas every time I moaned. Because he and Nick travelled in the back with me, they also got a whiff of the gas every time they put the mask on me. When we finally arrived neither man could stand on his feet.

'Your poor husband, he was so ill!' said the ward sister when I finally came to in the afternoon. They seemed to have more sympathy for him than for me and the baby. Michael, a big infant at more than 9 pounds, was battered and bruised after his difficult delivery and had to spend the first two days of his life in an incubator. I did not see my son until the third day.

'He's all right,' they said, 'we're taking good care of him, don't you worry.' But I did. There was little else I could do. I had to lie absolutely still on the tilted bed, uncomfortably stuck to the hard mattress and the rubber underlay. Because I had haemorrhaged I was 'packed' below and attached to various tubes at my top end. Did Michael and I come close to death that early morning in the theatre? I remember seeing a pair of dark brown eyes above a white face mask scrutinising me as I lay under some very bright circular lights. I remember someone saying, 'It doesn't matter now' in reply to a question a voice behind my head had asked. I remember thinking, That means it's too late. I remember feeling, I'm dying now. There was a black tunnel and a very bright light at the far end. I slid down that black tunnel. I was not frightened, and surprised that I was not.

When my baby was finally brought to me, the only part of him showing was his little red face, severely bruised at both cheekbones. His eyelids were swollen and his wee nose looked flattened. His skin felt damp when I kissed him. I wanted to unwrap him to see if he had the correct number of fingers and toes and everything else he was supposed to have, but Sister, a formidable woman, built like an unassailable fortress, firmly discouraged such frivolity. 'He's here to be breast-fed,' she announced. 'Get on with it. Ten minutes each side!'

I did not know how. It hurt to sit up on my stitches, it was embarrassing to bare all and my breasts felt hard and were sore. My baby did not know how either. We both got more and more dishevelled and hot and frustrated and did not achieve the required results at all. I was a failure as a mother. I snivelled. Sister came back, was not impressed by our poor performance and made this fact clear. She unwrapped Michael a bit – now I got a glimpse of his fingers and toes, which were all there, thank God – and masterfully clamped him onto me. The poor wee chap squirmed and mewed but finally drank a little. It hurt. 'Next feed in four hours,' she declared, as she bundled him away.

'You won't go home before the feeding routine is established. Have you bathed him yet?' I hadn't. It would probably be as difficult as breast-feeding. I was no good at either of these tasks. As a mother I was a total failure. I snivelled again. There was a lot of snivelling during the 10 days we spent at Queen Mary's. The new father, Nick, bewildered and worried by his changed status and responsibilities, departed for Roxburgh to his work, secretly relieved to be away from all that baby business, I suspected. We only knew one elderly couple in Dunedin, German-Jewish friends who kindly came to visit, but there was nobody I could share my feelings with, nobody I could ask for advice in confidence.

After seven days I was allowed up and instructed to go to the nursery to collect my baby and bathe him. I was appalled when I found Michael there, one of several identical bundles lying, wrapped up tight in white flannel, in a row of identical bassinets. The bundles were identifiable only by cards tied to the bassinets with blue or pink ribbon. Baby T. was bawling loudly, as were most other bundles. It is very difficult for a new mother to bathe a new baby for the first time. The infant is so slippery and so floppy and so small. You really need at least three hands to stop it from sliding under the water and drowning while you are trying to soap it all over and clean the tiny creases and hidden bits, then lift it out of the bath and onto the towel without it slipping through your fingers and splattering on the floor. Dressing it and pinning the nappies on securely without the safety pin sticking into either the baby or your fingers requires dexterity too.

On the day we were discharged, our Dunedin friends collected Michael and me to wait at his residence until Nick arrived to take us home. We had borrowed a cane travelling basket for Michael from a Dutch friend at the hydro. English friends took us home in their vintage car. At departure, having taken leave of our hosts, we got into the car and were just about to leave, when they asked, 'Haven't you forgotten something?' The something was our baby, sweetly asleep in his cane basket in the spare bedroom. Michael still likes to tell the story of how he was nearly abandoned by his parents at the tender age of 10 days.

Parenthood was a novel experience. We found that this was also a 24-hour commitment, seven days a week. At home we soon established the routine best suited to His Majesty the baby. Every hour of the day and night revolved around his well-being. We muddled through the first few colicky months with the help of Dinnefords and milk of magnesia. The Plunket nurse, much kinder than the sister at Queen Mary's had been, came at regular intervals to check on progress and give advice. Progress meant weight gain. This was measured by the ingenious method of parcelling the baby into his nappy, which was then hoisted aloft by means of a hook to which the scales were attached. I was always afraid of the dire consequences if the hook came adrift, but it never happened. We had the Plunket book, in which baby's progress was recorded. In the middle page was a graph showing the weight curve. Michael soon zoomed way up and over the average area and by six months he had zoomed right off the page, confirmation that we had, somewhere along the line, sussed the breast-feeding routine.

The winters were very cold at Roxburgh. Michael wore mittens and a woolly helmet to bed and when our hot water bottle fell onto the floor during the night, it was frozen solid in the morning. If the nappies were pegged out too soon or taken in too late, they froze into stiff shapes. You also had to take care to keep the nappies white and in spring you had to time the pegging out with cunning. On frosty mornings the smoke pots were lit under all the fruit trees in the orchards and a sooty, oily cloud hovered over the Clutha valley. It usually dispersed about 10 o'clock, but if the wind was blowing the wrong way, the cloud from the Alexandra orchards drifted down over the Roxburgh valley at 11, depositing a black sooty film over the nappies on the line.

In the 1960s there were no such labour-saving items as disposable nappies, baby wipes, canned baby foods and stretch-and-grow baby clothes; you did things the hard way. The first solids had to be sieved or mashed through a Mouli contraption. This was not too bad when it involved vegetables and fruit, but to process raw liver that way required a strong stomach and lots of maternal devotion. 'Raw liver is sooo beneficial to baby,' the Plunket nurse had said. To administer the equally beneficial daily dose of Lane's Emulsion (cod liver oil) to my reluctant infant was always a test of both our powers of perseverance.

And Michael grew. He sprouted blond hair, soft and fine as spring grass, grew baby teeth to smile and chew the side of his pram with, sat up by himself, fed himself very messily, to the distraction of his father, developed a determined little personality, talked baby talk and at 11 months toddled around and developed a taste for pebbles from the gravel paths around our house. This worried me at first, but the pebbles he swallowed pinged harmlessly into his potty a while later. I became totally absorbed in motherhood and that helped a little in dispelling the bouts of homesickness I so frequently experienced at that time. I still had one foot in each country, Germany and New Zealand, and felt I did not belong to either, yet was firmly anchored by my son to the obligation of making a success of family life for him and for Nick.

CHAPTER 33

Stratford

After five years of living and working at Roxburgh, we had fulfilled our obligation to the New Zealand government to work where and as directed and it was time to move on. The surveying work for the dam, now nearing completion, was scaling down. Nick had the option of staying with the Ministry of Works to work at the next dam projects, Lake Hawea and then Benmore, or trying for a position with a local body.

We had enjoyed the time at Roxburgh, we had made many good friends and had valued the security of steady employment and accommodation. It had been a good place in which to start our pioneering life and we were sad about leaving, but we wanted to find out how we would fare in 'real' New Zealand conditions, if we could hold our own without the benevolent umbrella of a government scheme. We scanned the newspaper situations vacant columns and wrote applications.

The county of Stratford in Taranaki offered Nick the position of engineer's assistant and so we set sail for the North Island. Nick's parents, who had settled in Lawrence, Central Otago, were disappointed that we were going so far away, because we had visited each other often during our stay in Roxburgh. Nick's father, a surveyor by profession, had been employed by the Ministry of Works to be part of the survey party that realigned and upgraded the main highway into Central Otago. He worked until he was 70.

Nick's parents were well received and respected by the good folk of Lawrence. They had saved hard and bought a little house in tree-lined Whitehaven Street, which led into the town centre. There they cultivated a large garden, grew raspberries, blackcurrants and vast quantities of vegetables, kept a few hens and a well-behaved cat. Faithful members of the Anglican congregation, they enjoyed the companionship of neighbours and friends, mostly retired folk like themselves. Nick's mother was famous for her baking. They continued their quiet life in Lawrence secure and content until Nick's father died many years later. His mother then came to live with us in Timaru.

'If you see the mountain, it's either just stopped raining, or it's about to start raining' is a true and popular saying in the rural town of Stratford, which is situated on the western slopes of the extinct volcano, Taranaki. Cone-shaped and snow-topped, the mighty mountain was then known as Egmont. The first British and Irish immigrants in the region cleared the bush off its lower slopes to establish pastures for dairy herds and sheep.

'A house goes with the job' we had been told and this was indeed so. Our new abode, 120 Celia Street, was an old wooden bungalow, endowed with a corrugated iron roof, a front porch, a toilet and wash-house out the back and the inevitable coal range. It was a Shacklock again, but a more upmarket version with an oven door of cream enamel and stippled green facings. The house had wooden floors, ceilings and walls, all stained a darkish brown, and was badly infested with borer beetles, which left little piles of wood dust everywhere. The wooden walls of the two bedrooms and the lounge had scrim stapled onto them and, a long time ago, floral wallpaper in hues of beige and brown had been pasted onto this. The scrim had become detached from the walls in many places, which created a billowing effect, and the borer had drilled numerous little exit holes through the wallpaper. To open the sash windows you manhandled one half of the frame up or down, not an easy task, as their pulley and rope system had perished, perhaps eaten by the borer?

The railway trunk line through the middle of the North Island to Ohura ran along Celia Street and the stop/go signal was right outside our gate. The trains used to clank and screech to a halt and then wait impatiently, hissing steam. If the wait was too long, they blew their whistle. This rattled our windows and panicked our cat, our dog and toddler Michael. Yes, we lived on the wrong side of the track in Stratford. The steep bank behind the garden sloped down to a muddy creek. Big eels lurked there, we were told. Behind the hedge to the south was the county yard, which housed graders, trucks, bulldozers and the workshop with all the paraphernalia needed for their maintenance. Another county house was next door to the north and a bit further along the road festered the town's rubbish dump.

The county engineer, the county clerk and their wives took a kindly interest in us. The engineer sold us two of his old easy chairs when he refurbished his lounge and the clerk offered me the job of cleaning the county office. This I did, every weekend for several months. It brought in a bit of much-needed cash to buy lino and Feltex to cover our floors, but a dedicated Mrs Mop I was not. I could cope with polishing the big table and leather-seated armchairs in the boardroom, and dusting the office furniture and oiling the dark brown lino of the floors was no problem, but scrubbing the men's toilets with their cracked and stained urinals was a challenge I did not rise to. A long-distance squirt of Harpic disinfectant and a swish with the soapy mop was all the cleaning they ever got.

Stratford in those days was a rather conservative and parochial town. Apart from us, not many foreigners lived there. We were a novelty, to be looked at, to be judged. I became conscious of this and determined that there would be nothing in my housekeeping, appearance or manners that could justify the comment: 'Typical German/Russian. What else could you expect!'

The people we met through Nick's work were kind to us but a little condescending and I was lonely. We needed friends, to be accepted into the community and not to be seen as a novelty. We attended the Anglican church where I warbled along in the choir and became a member of that venerable organisation, the League of Mothers. The meetings were much the same as those of the Women's Division in Roxburgh had been, with the addition of the set prayer we chanted at the beginning and end of each meeting. We joined a religious discussion group and there we found good friends with whom we are still in close contact. I went to an evening woodwork class where I sawed, planed and sanded planks ad infinitum until they turned into a sturdy bookshelf with a bedside cabinet at each end. They are hardly artefacts of beauty, but they have lasted and are now relegated to the garage where they hold animal remedies and garden sprays. I learned to sew, by correspondence. My first assignment, a tweed skirt with three pleats in the front and a zip in the back, travelled by post to and from my tutors for eight months before it was finished to their and my satisfaction.

After Michael started kindergarten I was able to take a part-time job as records clerk at Stratford Hospital. I enjoyed this immensely. True, once again I had to fill in and file little brown cards, transcribing patients' notes into codes, but reading patient records was fascinating – people had such interesting and sometimes gruesome ailments! Wrapping up specimen samples that came from the morgue in jars was a challenge: bits of a cancerous lung and a sad little baby's heart haunted me for a long time. Answering the phone and coping with the extension system was always interesting, especially for an emergency call.

But manning the counter was my favourite occupation. People came through the double doors with various requests: appointments to out patients' clinics, admission to hospital, visiting the wards, needing treatment at A and E (the accident and emergency department). All were meant to be 'received with calm efficiency' and most of them were, except for the chap who pinged the bell on the counter when I happened to be the only person in attendance. He had a stubbly, sunburnt face, topped by a red towelling hat, and wore khaki trousers tucked into gumboots and a checked shirt, unbuttoned to reveal a hairy chest. He looked burly, remarkably healthy and impatiently belligerent.

'Well, where do you want him?' he barked.

'Pardon?'

'What do you want done with him then? Come on, I haven't got all day.'

'Who?'

'The stiff I've got in my boot. Come on, girl, didn't they tell you?'

They had not and calm efficiency was no longer evident as I quavered, 'A corpse?', and sped along the corridor for help.

It turned out that he had pulled the deceased out from underneath a crashed motorbike that he found lying in a ditch beside a farm road. Not wanting to leave the body there, he had put it in the boot of his car and called at a nearby farmhouse to tell the 'silly woman' there to inform the hospital that he was bringing the body in. The poor soul, probably frightened out of her wits, had failed to do so.

I had some trouble with my use of language. It was somewhat colourful and I did not know the real meaning of many a phrase that tripped so lightly off my tongue. Once at an afternoon tea party, I gaily referred to my dear toddler son as 'the little sod'. There was an immediate and crashing silence in the lounge. One of the matrons present then informed me through pursed lips that 'sod' referred to sodomy. 'Sodom and Gomorrah,' she elaborated, and when it became obvious that I did not know what sodomy was, 'devious sexual practices.' I would dearly have loved to gain some more explicit information, but it was not forthcoming. Acutely aware of my faux pas, I blushingly apologised and refrained from using 'that word' ever again among the high society of Stratford.

Language became an issue about that time, not the choice of words but the decision of which should be the principal language for our child. Was he to grow up trilingual, feeling a little bit like a Russian, a bit like a German, but

169

alien in the country of his birth? We decided he was to grow up a Kiwi, identify himself as belonging here, for better or worse, and so we decided on English as the communication language in our home.

Now, nearly half a century later, I can answer 'yes' to the question, 'Did we succeed in raising our three youngsters as Kiwis?' They all feel that this is their home, that this is their country, that they belong here. Their partners are New Zealanders, our first grandchild is a little fair dinkum Kiwi chick. And yet all three tell me now that, at school, they were acutely aware of being different, sometimes embarrassed and upset about incidents when they were identified as belonging to a people, German or Russian, whose actions the Social Studies syllabus classified as deplorable. All three voluntarily learned German, both our daughters learned Russian/Ukrainian and all three travelled to Europe to find their roots. They now enjoy being a little different; having exotic parentage has become fashionable.

In 1956 we received notice that we were eligible to become naturalised New Zealand citizens. For Nick this posed no problem since he and his parents had been classed as stateless. Like many other exiles of imperial Russia, who fled their homeland when it became the Soviet Union, they had been issued with a 'Nansen passport' (after Fridtjof Nansen, the Norwegian explorer, humanitarian and Nobel Peace Prize winner who suggested the concept). This internationally recognised passport enabled stateless people to cross the borders of countries belonging to the League of Nations, then, later, the United Nations.

Nick wanted to become a New Zealander; after all, he had felt that this country was the right one to bring his family to. It had been a good move, we were, and still are, happy with our chosen land. Our son, Michael, born in Dunedin, was a New Zealand citizen already. I did not think that becoming a New Zealander by naturalisation would be a problem for me either, because New Zealand allows dual citizenship; I thought I would retain German citizenship as well. Only 30 years later did I find out that I had lost my German citizenship, because I had not formally applied to keep it when I became a New Zealand citizen. Before even countenancing the issue of a passport, German bureaucracy demanded costly and extensive proof that I was of pure German descent for at least three generations. A farce, considering my background!

And so, in 1956, we became New Zealand citizens, at a formal ceremony held in the council chambers of Stratford. Hats and gloves were de rigueur and the mayor wore his chain of office. We swore allegiance to Her Majesty the Queen, on the Bible, and afterwards the mayor gave a little speech: 'Congratulations to you both, new citizens of New Zealand and of the Borough of Stratford, Taranaki in particular. We welcome people like you, people of good European stock.' Taranaki, dairy farming, herds of well-bred, productive Friesians originating from Friesland, North Germany. Good European stock, like Nick and me. I had to suppress a giggle and the desire to say 'moo' when shaking hands with the mayor.

With that ceremony I became a New Zealand citizen, a certified, legalised import, a Kiwi by choice, by naturalisation, by fate? If so, it was a kind fate that sent me to Aotearoa. This most beautiful country at the end of the earth owns us now, has captured our hearts. Nick and I enjoy the freedom and tranquillity of a relaxed and simple lifestyle. We value the kindness, the practicality and the eccentricity of our fellow Kiwis. My accent will always identify me as a newcomer but it has never been a barrier to friendships, or to the sense of belonging here. It is true that this sense of being accepted did not just happen. It was something to be worked at, requiring hard physical and mental effort over many years. And then it came unexpectedly, like a gift. One morning, looking at South Canterbury's Hunters Hills, silhouetted blue against a brilliant sky of orange and red hues, I suddenly knew, 'Yes, this is where I belong now, this is where I want to be for the rest of my life.' Homesickness for the country of my birth, Germany, faded away at that moment.

I have a picture in my mind of a leaf floating on water, at first in a sunlit stream that is bubbling over pebbles, secure within its green banks. Then the stream enters a dark gorge, cascades over rocks, becomes a waterfall and tumbles down, down into a dark pool. The leaf is swept along, swirling in the turbulent waters. Steep, jagged rocks tower over the stream now as it flows through crevices, over boulders, around the debris of fallen trees. Finally the stream overcomes its tribulations, emerges into the foothills, carries the leaf with it to sunlit pastures. It has become a river now, stronger, deeper, slower moving. It still carries the leaf on its way to its destination, the shining waters of the ocean. I am that leaf.

Postscript

L ove you, Oma, bye,' says granddaughter Jana as she firmly plants her
podgy finger on the OFF button, terminating our telephone conversation.
At two years old she will be busy all day, toddling from one exciting and chal-
lenging activity to the next, eager, confident, happy, secure.

A warm glow of happiness persists after I replaced the receiver. Jana, the
daughter of Katerina and Mark, has inherited her mother's warm-hearted, out-
going personality and deep blue eyes, her father's energy, perseverance and the
little cleft in her chin, which already gives her a determined air. Loved and
cherished by all members of our extended family, she enjoys a sunny childhood living atop a bush-clad ridge just north of Wellington.

Her mother, Katerina, our youngest daughter, was born at Te Kuiti in the
King Country where we lived for five years after the time we spent in Stratford.
Before she was one year old we moved to Timaru, where she and her siblings,
Sonja and Michael grew up, progressing through kindergarten, primary and
secondary schools in the city. Charming and imaginative by nature, Katerina
was always surrounded by playmates throughout her childhood and she and
her husband Mark still extend hospitality to a wide variety of friends.

The very close bond that exists between Katerina and me has helped me
over many a rough patch I encountered when writing this book. I am grateful
for the loving support she continues to give me.

Katerina, Sonja and Michael have always been harbingers of joy and love
for me. We are fortunate indeed that as mature adults they and their partners
continue to share their feelings and thoughts with Nick and me.

Lupins from New Zealand will bloom this summer on the slope behind a grey
apartment building in the centre of the city of Kiev in the Ukraine. Splashes of

pink, blue, purple and white, just like the lupins along the road that runs through the Mackenzie Country to Mount Cook. Our daughter Sonja who, with her husband Richard, has been living in Kiev for the past two years, planted the seeds sent from here. Sonja, born in Stratford after we were naturalised, was a chubby and determined infant of sunny disposition. Solnushka (little sunshine) Nick called her, when she was a toddler. Caring and compassionate, Sonja continues to look after creatures great and small, feeding a colony of wild cats and rescuing numerous 'street dogs' in Kiev.

It was Sonja who wanted to know details about her grandfather's involvement with Hitler when we stood near the Feldherrnhalle in Munich in 1984. I could not tell her then, because I had not resolved my hurt and pain. Sonja understood. Later, when I started to write my story, she, like Michael and Katerina, encouraged me to persevere with the task.

Michael has returned to his birthplace, Dunedin, after travelling extensively overseas, and lives in a mutually loving and supportive relationship with Amanda. They are at present remodelling their villa into a 'dream house', a project they hope to finish in time for their wedding.

All our children share my love for animals, but Michael extends this to an affection for creepy crawlies. As a little boy in Te Kuiti he was enamoured of the large green frogs that inhabited the swamp adjoining our garden. One afternoon I found 68 of his croaking, jumping, slimy friends inhabiting the laundry tub. Told to shift them, he put them into the bath. Later in Timaru he shared his bedroom with a colony of little black ants that were supposed to live in their ants nest, safely confined between two sheets of glass, but emerged, marching in long columns along the bookshelves and the window sills. Their daily exodus was of concern to me, but Michael assured me that his six-legged friends returned to their abode every night, and they did so indeed, because he fed them sugar in their nest.

We moved to Timaru, Te Maru, place of shelter, 36 years ago and it is still our home town. We spent the first few years in the city, where Nick kept the roads and bridges of the Levels County up to scratch, I taught German and English at Timaru's high schools and at adult education classes, studying for the necessary qualifications at night. The children attended school and somehow we found the time to enjoy and care for the menagerie of pets that enriched our lives: goldfish, tropical fish, frogs, ants, a budgie, 31 guinea pigs, two cats, a

Dachshund and later a German Shepherd, up to five pet lambs in and around our house and three horses in a rented paddock up the road.

The move to 11 hectares of rolling country a few kilometres out of town was not only a practical solution, but also the fulfilment of a dream. Now we could see our horses from the bedroom window, we could realise our farming ambitions, we could plant trees, we could establish a peaceful place of shelter for our children and their children. We built a house, a barn, a garage and sheds. We divided the land into paddocks. We fenced, established shelter belts, planted more than 2000 trees, made a drive, an orchard, a garden, a vegetable patch, put in troughs, erected sheepyards, made hay. We farmed black and coloured sheep, beef cattle, Angora goats. We kept hens and peacocks. We trekked far and wide on our horses. That there were a lot of chores to be done is almost an understatement, but our three youngsters pitched in wholeheartedly and somehow, often with the enthusiastic help of 'townie' friends, we muddled through, and learned, and became quite proficient.

Nick and I still enjoy the tranquillity and beauty of our small slice of paradise and cherish every day we can be here. We no longer farm the place, but Indi the faithful old pony is in the front paddock. Thirty years old, with hardly a tooth in his head, he contentedly gums his way through finely sliced carrots, chaff and pony nuts. A flock of 13 peacocks struts around the paddocks and the whanau of pukeko fiercely defend their territory down at the pond. Pavarotti the bellbird serenades us morning and evening. He has Nick trained to keep his supply of sugar water at the required level. Five gregarious fantails flit in and out of the house and garage, chattering rapidly as they swoop to catch insects.

The most important 'people' on the place are definitely the two giant Schnauzers, Max and Phoebe. Always right beside us, insisting on a healthy routine of walking, resting and eating at regular intervals, they ensure their and our wellbeing. Big, black, powerful dogs, they are sometimes a bit of a worry when they get over-enthusiastic in defending us and the property or chasing anything that moves, but their motives are always pure, they assure us with wet whiskery kisses, rapid wagging of their stumpy tails and honest looks from melting brown eyes. They love us as unreservedly as we love them.

In June 2000, Nick and I celebrated our golden wedding anniversary and were able to say thank you to our extended family and all the dear friends who have given us love and support throughout our 49 years of life in New Zealand.